SPECIAL NEEDS in the early years

Sensory difficulties

IDENTIFYING AND SUPPORTING NEEDS • ACTIVITIES COVERING EARLY LEARNING GOALS • WORKING WITH PARENTS

DR HANNAH MORTIMER

Author
Dr Hannah Mortimer

Editor
Lesley Sudlow

Assistant Editor
Saveria Mezzana

Series Designers
Sarah Rock/Anna Oliwa

Designer
Heather C Sanneh

Illustrations
Shelagh McNicholas

Cover artwork
Claire Henley

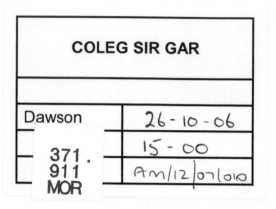
Acknowledgements
Qualifications and Curriculum Authority for the use of extracts from the
QCA/DfEE document *Curriculum Guidance for the Foundation Stage*
© 2000, Qualifications and Curriculum Authority.

The publishers wish to thank Makaton Vocabulary Development Project for their help in
reproducing the Makaton illustrations in this book and Royal National Institute for the Blind
for activity ideas and resources.
Every effort has been made to trace copyright holders and the publishers apologize for any
inadvertent omissions.

Text © 2002, Hannah Mortimer
© 2002, Scholastic Ltd

Designed using Adobe Pagemaker

Published by Scholastic Ltd, Villiers House,
Clarendon Avenue, Leamington Spa, Warwickshire CV32 5PR

Visit our website at www.scholastic.co.uk

Printed by Alden Group Ltd, Oxford

1 2 3 4 5 6 7 8 9 0   2 3 4 5 6 7 8 9 0 1

British Library Cataloguing-in-Publication Data A catalogue record for this book is
available from the British Library.

ISBN 0590 53565 X

Sensory difficulties

KNOWLEDGE AND UNDERSTANDING OF THE WORLD

PHYSICAL DEVELOPMENT

CREATIVE DEVELOPMENT

PHOTOCOPIABLES

INTRODUCTION

Seeing and hearing are senses that are important channels for early learning. When children's vision and hearing do not develop normally, it is necessary for practitioners to identify and support their difficulties as soon as possible.

The aims of the series

There is now a revised *Code of Practice* for the identification and assessment of special educational needs. Early years settings will therefore require guidance on what these changes mean to them. In addition, the QCA document *Curriculum Guidance for the Foundation Stage* emphasizes the key role that early years practitioners play in identifying needs and responding quickly to them. While most early years practitioners feel that an inclusive approach is the best one for all the children concerned, they still need advice on what an inclusive early years curriculum might actually 'look like' in practice.

Within this series, there are books on helping children with most kinds of special needs:
- behavioural and emotional difficulties
- speech and language difficulties
- learning difficulties
- physical and co-ordination difficulties
- autistic spectrum difficulties
- medical difficulties
- sensory difficulties.

There is also a *Special Needs Handbook* to accompany the whole series. It provides general guidance and more detail on how to assess, plan for, teach and monitor children with SEN in early years settings.

Many early years groups will, at some point, include children who have sensory difficulties. These children will suffer from mild to severe visual or hearing impairment, including fluctuating hearing loss and

glue ear, and a few children may be registered blind or be deaf. This book will help all early years professionals to recognize and understand such difficulties and to provide inclusive activities for the children concerned. Market research has shown that early years practitioners would welcome practical advice and guidelines for these children.

How to use the book

Chapter 1 provides an introduction to the requirements under the revised *Code of Practice* for SEN as it relates to children who have sensory difficulties affecting their hearing, vision or both. This is only a brief guide, with close reference made to the series handbook for more information. There is also a reminder of the requirements of the Early Learning Goals (QCA) and curriculum guidelines

across each Area of Learning. The need for individual education plans (IEPs) for those children who have SEN is introduced, and advice is given on how to meet SEN in an inclusive way. Pointers are provided for developing positive partnerships and relationships with parents and carers, and some of the outside agencies that you may need to liaise with are also referred to.

Chapter 2 looks more closely at the requirements of children who have sensory difficulties. It gives advice on the kinds of conditions and needs of those children, and explains how these difficulties arise, what you should be noticing in the children in your setting, the problems encountered by the children and the educational implications. Suggestions are also provided on how to look for special opportunities for promoting sensory development linked to the early years curriculum. Encouragement is given for you to try a range of approaches and make use of the full extent of resources and activities available in your setting.

Chapters 3 to 8 are activity chapters with each one related to one of the Areas of Learning: Personal, social and emotional development; Communication, language and literacy; Mathematical development; Knowledge and understanding of the world; Physical development and Creative development. Every chapter contains ten activities, each with a learning objective for all the children (with or without SEN) and an individual learning target for any children who might have any one of a range of sensory difficulties. The activities target different kinds of difficulties, in the hope that early years practitioners will be able to develop a flexible approach to planning inclusive activities. Each child and set of needs are unique, so you will need to adapt and develop the ideas to fit your situation rather than use them as 'recipes'. It is suggested that you read through all the chapters for their general ideas, then select activities as and when you need them as part of your curriculum planning. Each individual learning target is followed by an eye symbol ◉ if the activity is particularly suitable for children who have visual impairment, or an ear symbol 👂 if the activity would be especially helpful for children with hearing impairment.

The activities give recommendations for the appropriate group size, a list of what you need, a description of what to do, any special support that might be necessary for a child with special needs, ideas for extending the activity for more able children, and suggestions for links with home. Again, these guidelines are flexible and you should take into account the needs of the children and your particular setting.

Although this book relates to the early years and SEN procedures followed in England, the general guidance on individual planning, positive behaviour management and activities will be equally relevant to practitioners in other countries.

How children's hearing usually develops

In most circumstances, developing babies soon become aware of sounds: they move their arms and legs vigorously to music or voice, and gradually turn their eyes and head towards the source of the sound. It is soon apparent to the parents or carers that their baby can hear them when they enter a room or are startled when there is a loud noise. A child of nine to 19 months learns how to make sounds, for example,

exploring small objects and toys by rattling, shaking and banging. They take a special interest in voices and start to leave gaps when they are spoken to by replying with babbles or first words of their own. In time, they build up an understanding of the objects and people around them from how they look, what they do, how they sound and how they feel or taste. All of these early experiences become linked in a co-ordinated way and help young children to make sense of the world around them.

Children with impaired hearing

When hearing does not develop normally, for whatever reason, there will be gaps in the links that the child is making. They may miss out on important information just at the stage when language would normally develop and links would be made. They are likely to have limited vocabulary and fail to understand abstract words such as 'more' and 'heavy'. This is because they will not have picked up so readily the words that link with their actions. They are also likely to have less success in conversation and language as they may speak unclearly, or fail to respond appropriately because they have not heard. Therefore communication between the child and other adults and children may not flow in a meaningful way. The child with hearing impairment may quickly lose confidence and become isolated or quiet.

How children's vision usually develops

A newborn baby has a limited focus but soon learns to fixate on close faces. They develop an interest in bright and colourful objects as well as in people, and it is evident that the baby begins to turn their eyes and head to follow a moving toy or person. After some initial wide swipes, a planned and co-ordinated attempt to grab, strike and later pick up will follow. A developing toddler is then ready to begin to make the important links between seeing, hearing and interacting with familiar object and toys.

Children with impaired vision

For a child whose vision does not develop normally, these early links are going to be very different. The child will not be able to explore their world actively when they have no idea what is beyond their immediate surroundings. It will be impossible for them to play imaginatively with a doll's house if it feels nothing like the real thing.

After all, to a sighted child, a miniature house and its contents at least 'look' like the real thing.

By understanding the differences in the way that children with sensory impairment learn, you will be able to plan more effective and inclusive approaches. This is explained in more detail in Chapter 2 (pages 15–24).

Using a wide variety of resources in your setting

The activities described in this book will enable you to make use of a wide range of resources and materials available in your setting. There are ideas for art and craft, story time, physical play, exploring and finding out. Special use is made of circle-time approaches with young children since these have shown to be very effective in building children's self-esteem and confidence, as well as in teaching them how to demonstrate new skills within a group.

Research has shown that using a regular music circle time can enhance looking, listening, joining in and confidence, both within circle time and beyond, and many of the activities in this book use a musical approach, too. Some children who are reluctant to receive individual physiotherapy may still enjoy doing the same exercises to music as part of a group action game. Because children with visual impairment face particular challenges during physical activities, there is a predominance of activities targeted at children with these difficulties in the chapter on Physical development (pages 65–74).

Links with home

All the activities suggest ways of keeping closely in touch with home. By sharing activities with parents and carers, you can also play a role in helping the parents or carers of a child who has sensory difficulties to follow approaches that will make everyone feel a lot more encouraged at home.

Providing special support for children with sensory difficulties

Make sure that a child with sensory difficulties is accessing the full range of your early years provision. Clearly this cannot happen if the child is isolated in any way or withdrawn from the group regularly, and this is another reason for collecting ideas for 'inclusive' group activities. 'Support' does not have to mean individual one-to-one attention. Instead, it can mean playing alongside a child or watching them, so as to encourage new learning, staying 'one step ahead' of any problem times, such as when the other children are moving around quickly or there is a lot of background noise, and sometimes teaching the child in small groups.

THE LEGAL REQUIREMENTS

This chapter explains the revised *Code of Practice* and provides advice on meeting special educational needs. There are ideas for making individual education plans for children with sensory difficulties and for working closely with parents, carers and other professionals.

The *Code of Practice* for SEN

The *Code of Practice* for SEN is a guide for school governors, registered early years providers and local education authorities (LEAs), relating to the practical help that they can give to children with special educational needs. It recommends that schools and early years providers should identify children's needs and take action to meet those needs as early as possible, working together with parents and carers. The aim is to enable all pupils with special needs to reach their full potential, to be included fully in their school communities and to make a successful transition to adulthood. The Code gives guidance to schools and early years providers, but it does not tell them what they must do in every case.

The contents of the revised SEN *Code of Practice* are described in more detail in the *Special Needs Handbook* in this series.

The underlying principles for early years settings

All young children have a right to a broad and balanced curriculum that enables them to make maximum progress towards the Early Learning Goals. Early years practitioners must recognize, identify and meet SEN within their settings. There will be a range of needs and a range of provision to meet those needs. Most children with SEN will be in a local mainstream early years group or class, even those who have 'statements of SEN' (see page 10). Parents, children, early years settings, and support services should work as partners in planning for and meeting SEN.

The *Code of Practice* is designed to enable SEN to be identified early and addressed. These SEN will normally be met in the local mainstream setting, although some children may need extra consideration or help to be able to fully access the early years curriculum.

Using flexible approaches

It is recognized that good practice can take many forms, and early years practitioners are encouraged to adopt a flexible and graduated response to the SEN of individual children. This approach acknowledges that there is a continuum of SEN and, where necessary, brings increasing specialist

expertise on board if the child is experiencing continuing difficulties. Once a child's SEN have been identified, the practitioners should intervene through 'Early Years Action'. This intervention is co-ordinated by one person within the setting who has been designated as the SEN link person, the Special Educational Needs Co-ordinator (SENCO). However, each adult in the setting shares the responsibility of intervening to support the child. This book concentrates on intervening and setting targets for children who have sensory difficulties.

Early Years Action Plus

When reviewing the child's progress and the help that they are receiving, the practitioners might decide to seek alternative approaches to learning through the involvement of outside support services. These interventions are known as 'Early Years Action Plus'. The SENCO continues to take a leading role, working closely with the member of staff responsible for the child, and:

● draws on the advice from outside specialists, for example, specialist teachers for children with hearing or visual impairments, and educational psychologists

● ensures that the child and their parents or carers are consulted and kept informed

● makes sure that an individual education plan is drawn up, incorporating the specialist advice, and that it is included in the curriculum planning for the whole setting

● monitors and reviews the child's progress with outside specialists

● keeps the Head of the setting informed.

Statements of SEN

For very few children, the help provided by Early Years Action Plus will still not be sufficient to ensure satisfactory progress, even when it has run over several review periods. The practitioners, external professionals and parents or carers may then decide to ask the LEA to consider carrying out a statutory assessment of the child's SEN. The LEA must decide quickly whether or not it has the 'evidence' to indicate that a statutory assessment is necessary for a child. It is then responsible for co-ordinating a statutory assessment and will call for the various reports required from the early years teacher (usually a support teacher, early years practitioner or LEA nursery teacher), an educational psychologist, a doctor (who will also gather evidence from any therapist working with the child) and the Social Services Department (if involved). It will also ask the parents or carers to submit their own views and evidence.

Once the LEA has collected the evidence, they might decide to issue a 'statement of SEN' for the child. Only children with severe and long-standing SEN will go on to receive a statement – this is approximately two per cent of children. There are various rights of appeal in the cases of disagreement, and the LEA can provide information about these.

Requirements of the Early Learning Goals

Registered early years providers are also expected to deliver a broad and balanced curriculum across the six Areas of Learning as defined in the *Curriculum Guidance for the Foundation Stage* (QCA). The six Areas of Learning are Personal, social and emotional development, Communication, language and literacy; Mathematical development; Knowledge and understanding of the world; Physical development and Creative development. This paves the way for children's early learning to be followed through into Baseline Assessment measures on entry to school and into National Curriculum assessment for school-age children. It is expected that the integration of these will contribute to the earlier identification of children who are experiencing difficulties in making progress.

The Early Learning Goals have been carefully set into context so that they are seen as an aid to planning ahead rather than as an early years curriculum to replace 'learning through play'. Effective early years education needs a relevant curriculum as well as practitioners who understand and are able to implement it. To this end, practical examples of Stepping Stones towards the Goals are provided in the detailed curriculum guidance.

Within this book, each activity is linked to a learning objective for the whole group, and also to an individual learning target for any child who has sensory difficulties. The ideas suggested can be applied equally well to the documents on pre-school education published for Scotland, Wales and Northern Ireland.

The need for individual education plans

One characteristic of Early Years Action for the child with SEN is the writing of the individual education plan. This is a detailed plan that aims to ensure that the child will make progress. An example of an IEP is shown on page 12 and a photocopiable pro forma appears on page 85. This plan should be reviewed regularly with the child's parents or carers. The plan should be seen as an integrated aspect of the curriculum planning for the whole group and should only include that information which is additional to or different from the differentiated early years curriculum that is in place for all the children.

Case study: Sam

Sam is nearly four years old. When he was a baby, his family noticed that he did not seem to hear them when they came into his room. He started to babble, but this was mainly in vowel sounds, and no clear words developed. He was always crying with earache and the doctors found that he had recurrent ear infections.

Sam was assessed by the community doctor who found him to have a moderate to

Individual education plan

| **Name:** Sam | **Early Years Action Plus** |

Nature of sensory difficulty: Sam has a moderate to severe hearing loss. He has been fitted with a radio hearing aid.

Who else is involved?
Jenny D – Speech and Language Therapist; Simone W – Advisory Teacher for the Hearing Impaired; Dr G – Ear, Nose and Throat Consultant.

Action
1 Seeking further information
Simone is to visit us to advise on the use of the radio aid and on the implications of Sam's difficulty.

2 Seeking training or support
Jenny has suggested a programme of activities for encouraging speech for Sam.

3 Observations and assessments
Simone will visit the nursery once a fortnight to check on Sam's equipment, work individually with him, advise on helpful approaches and materials, assess how he is responding to his aids and help the staff with their planning, assessment and monitoring.

4 Encouraging learning and sensory development
● *What exactly are the new skills that we wish to teach?*
We want to teach Sam to speak more clearly and to understand abstract vocabulary.
● *How will we teach them?*
We will use a range of natural play opportunities to see which abstract words Sam responds to and we will note down those that he does not, planning practical opportunities for building them. We will follow the programme set by Jenny D.
We will approach the committee about carpeting and curtains for the playroom in order to absorb background noise.
● *What opportunities will we make for helping Sam to generalize and practise these skills throughout the session?*
We will play alongside Sam in a small group to build on and extend his new learning.
● *How will we make sure that Sam is fully included in the early years curriculum?*
We will plan at least one activity each session targeted especially for Sam's needs, and we will also make sure that we support him during all the other activities.

Help from parents
A diary will run between nursery, the speech and language therapist and home, so that everyone can work on the same language activities and goals.

Targets for this term
● Sam will play for five minutes on the car mat with one other child, with an adult repeating and developing what he is saying to help the conversation.
● Sam will be able to use phrases of at least three words that can be clearly understood by other children.
● Sam will look and listen to a story within a large group when the leader wears the radio aid.
● Sam will show which of two objects is 'longer', 'shorter', 'more than', 'less than', 'higher' or 'lower'.
● *How will we measure whether we have achieved these targets?*
Evaluation of Sam's progress against these targets will be made fortnightly.

Review meeting with parents
In six weeks' time. Invite the speech and language therapist, teacher for children with hearing impairment and the SENCO for our school.

severe hearing loss. The Ear, Nose and Throat Consultant carried out investigations and found that his deafness was due to a mixture of central neurological damage (the sound signals were not all being received from ear to brain) and conductive loss (the sound vibrations were not being conducted through his middle ear due to a build up of glue-like fluid). Sam went into hospital when he was just three to have grommets inserted. These helped to drain his middle ear and the sounds to conduct more easily. He was also given hearing aids to help him to make best use of his remaining hearing.

These investigations took time, and Sam's hearing was affected at a vital stage for learning language. It is likely that Sam missed valuable opportunities to learn to speak clearly and to link actions and words in a way that helps him to understand abstract concepts. The teacher for children with hearing impairment has become involved and Sam is receiving speech and language therapy. His needs are being monitored through Early Years Action Plus.

Sam's nursery teacher must therefore draw up an individual education plan at least every term with advice from their Special Educational Needs Co-ordinator, and meet regularly with Sam's parents and outside professionals to review it.

Working with parents and carers

Parents and carers often ask how they can help their child at home when areas of concern are expressed by the early years setting. They might also approach you with their own concerns that they need you to address with them. Parents are the primary educators of their

children and should be included from the start as an essential part of the whole-group approach to meeting a child's needs. They have expert knowledge on their own child and you will need to create an ethos which shows how much this information is valued and made use of. Information sharing is important and is a two-way process.

The following are some practical ways of involving the parents or carers in meeting their child's needs:

● Make a personal invitation to them. For various reasons, parents and carers do not always call in to the setting on a daily basis. It is often helpful to invite them in to share information about their child's achievements in an informal way, or, if possible, to arrange a home visit.

● Draw the parents or carers' attention to a specific display in your setting, where examples of their child's work can be seen.

● Show the parents or carers what their child has already achieved and improvements in their development within the setting. At the same time, do not make them feel too despondent if there have not been improvements at home. Use the 'good news' as a hope for positive changes to come.

● Encourage the child to show their parents or carers what they can do, what they can say or what they have learned.

● Ask parents and carers for their opinions, by allowing opportunities for them to contribute information and share experiences. It is often helpful to set a regular time aside when other demands will not intrude.

● Thank parents and carers regularly for their support.

● Celebrate success with parents and carers. This will ensure an ongoing positive partnership.

● Use a home–setting diary to keep in touch.

● A two-way system of sharing information about a child's success, experiences and opportunities can help in supporting the child.

Working with outside agencies

When assessing and working with a young child who has special needs, an outside professional might be involved in helping staff to monitor and meet the child's needs. For children with sensory difficulties, this is likely to be a sensory support teacher, a specialist doctor, a Portage home visitor (see page 96) or members of the local Child Development Team. The type of advice and support available will vary with local policies and practices.

Sensory support teachers are employed by the LEA and aim to work towards helping the child to reach their maximum potential. Following assessment and liaison with the specialist doctor, they will work closely

with the parents or carers and with early years practitioners to establish appropriate goals for the child. This individually planned programme might cover careful positioning and lighting, advice and support, methods of non-verbal communication and any special equipment needed to ensure best use of residual vision or hearing.

Sometimes, it may be yourself who will be identifying a child's sensory difficulties for the first time. Guidance regarding this is given in the next chapter. You might reach the stage where you feel that outside professional help is needed. Usually, a request for help from outside agencies is likely to follow a decision taken by the SENCO, colleagues and parents or carers when reviewing a child's progress in the setting. Questions may be asked, for example, 'Has progress been made?', 'How do the parents or carers feel?', 'Do we need more information and advice on the child's needs from outside?' and so on.

HELPING CHILDREN WITH SENSORY DIFFICULTIES

This chapter considers the needs of children who have difficulties in seeing or hearing. There are practical ideas for supporting these children across all Areas of Learning and for making them welcome.

The conditions covered

In this book, you will find information and ideas to help you to meet the needs of children with a range of sensory impairments. There are ideas for supporting children who have hearing impairment, and ideas for supporting children who have visual impairment. Each child's needs are individual to them, depending on the nature of the impairment, your circumstances and their experience. It would be impossible to prescribe activities that suit everybody in a 'cookery-book style'. The purpose of this chapter is to provide the background information that may be needed in order to dip into and develop the activities to suit the children that you are working with.

Supporting children with visual and hearing impairments

It is important to remember that each child with a sensory impairment is first and foremost a child who is developing individually, no matter how serious the impairment. Hearing and vision are major sources of information and these children may not have had the same opportunities as others to pick up and integrate information when playing. Therefore planning is required to teach structured opportunities to compensate for this. Learning through other senses may not be as quick or as complete as it would have been if the child had been able to see or hear clearly. Consequently, these children need time, opportunities and understanding if they are to make good progress. They are also likely to be less confident than their peers since social communication flows better for children without such difficulties.

Visual difficulties

There are visual difficulties associated with not being able to focus clearly. These difficulties may hardly affect the child at all, or they may be so serious that the child finds it hard to see clearly even with spectacles. There are children who have difficulty in seeing people and objects clearly unless they are close up and well lit. These children are near-sighted, or 'myopic', and may have been prescribed spectacles to

wear. Other children can only see clearly at a distance. They may be far-sighted, or 'presbyopic', and again have to wear spectacles. Parents and carers should be able to tell you when it is important for their children to wear spectacles.

For some children, the difficulty is that they cannot co-ordinate the movement of their eyes when tracking and examining things. They might also have a squint and may need a patch to make one eye more dominant. Parents and carers should be able to tell you when the patch should be worn and for how long each session.

Colour-blindness

Some children are unable to distinguish certain colours. 'Colour-blindness' can take different forms. Occasionally, children can mask this difficulty because they can still match and sort different shades and hues of colour. If you suspect that a child has colour-blindness, ask the parents or carers if there is a history of colour-blindness in the family and request help and advice from the school nurse or health visitor. Alternatively, the parents or carers can take their child to see an optician or optometrist.

Complex forms of visual difficulty

Some children have patches of blindness or even tunnel vision that restricts their field of vision. Some children's sight is so restricted that they are effectively 'blind'. Approximately five per cent of children with visual impairment go on to use Braille for reading and writing. Some children have no pigment in the iris of their eye, and this makes it very hard for them to tolerate bright light. For this complex group of children, it is likely that a qualified teacher for visually impaired children will already be involved from the Local Education Authority and they will be able to advise you about how to support the children. Most of the activities in this book that support children with visual difficulties are aimed at children who have significant and long-term visual difficulties and who are therefore on your setting's SEN register.

How you can help

A child with visual impairment needs the same play opportunities as any other child. If you find out about their individual needs, you can then plan ahead and compensate for any missed opportunities that they might have had because of their sensory impairment.

● Choose brightly coloured toys and play things that attract visual attention.

● Children with visual impairment may need more contrast than usual, for example, dark objects against a light background or vice versa.

● Look for play things that make a sound or are interesting to feel. The RNIB (see page 95) produces a toy catalogue full of ideas for toys that

can be enjoyed through more than one sense, and suggests the ages of children for which they are suitable.

● Make sure that your areas are well lit. For children whose eyes are very light-sensitive, you may also need to plan shady areas for comfort.

● Keep floors free from unnecessary clutter and obstacles. Although children who are blind will learn to feel for objects with their feet, this skill takes time and you need to be on your guard for the worst traps.

● Take the usual precautions to ensure safety, for example, safety plugs on sockets, removing trailing wires, guarding hot radiators, supervising climbing apparatus and securing outside doors.

● Be aware that doors can easily trap fingers or be walked into. Consider wedging doors open if they are not fire doors, or keeping them firmly shut. Fix polystyrene strips to door edges and cut away spaces around hinges to avoid trapping fingers.

● Choose sounds to go with different areas of the setting. Wind chimes can inform a child not only of where the door is, but also where other things are in relation to the door, for example, 'The water tray is near the door'.

● Have well-defined areas for keeping toys and materials, so that a child with visual difficulties can always find them. Textured and shaped mats on shelves can tell blind children where something belongs. Textured floor areas will enable them to 'map' the playroom and remember where things are.

● Make sure that your large construction equipment area is clearly indicated for apparatus and physical play, so that children with poor

sight are not bumped into in the quieter areas.

● Where possible, use carpeting, curtains and soft furnishings to absorb sound, thereby making sounds easier to hear and locate.

● Be aware that children whose vision is restricted may not see you coming (even spectacles restrict range of vision). Approach them from the front, if possible, and say the child's name so that they can identify you from your voice.

● Always use the child's name when you start to talk, and mention who you are, too, for example, 'Hello Jake, it's Carole and I've come to play with you. Here comes Raj as well'. Use all the other children's names as well so that the child who cannot see well knows who you are addressing.

● Sit the children with near-sight close to the front during discussions and at story time. Use concrete props, such as a character to hold or a story sack to explore, as well as pictures.

● Borrow picture books with large print from your local library. The librarians will also be able to tell you about their range of tactile books, smell books and interactive books.

● As a group, sing songs that will help a child with little vision to get to know everyone's name

quickly. An idea for a name song is given in the activity 'Close encounters' on page 31.

● Consider slightly sloping surfaces to make table-top activities easier to see. Attach white tape to the edge of tables and shelves to make it easier for a child with limited vision to see.

Hearing difficulties

Many early years children suffer from temporary, fluctuating or even permanent hearing loss. Approximately 840 children a year are born with a permanent hearing impairment, and thousands more will have a temporary loss. Temporary hearing loss can be caused by colds leading to ear infections. There may be a redness around the ear, the child

might have earache and a fever, and they may seem less responsive to sound than usual. You might also notice that a child is speaking rather louder than usual. Sometimes a build-up of mucus in the middle ear prevents the sounds from being transmitted properly, which leads to conductive deafness. This is known as 'glue ear' and is often treated at hospital by draining the mucus and then inserting grommets.

'Sensori-neural deafness' usually means that sounds are not being processed correctly in the inner ear. Sometimes this can follow after having rubella, mumps or meningitis. This is likely to be a permanent hearing impairment.

In the case of 'mixed deafness', the child may have a combination of conductive and sensori-neural

hearing impairment. Very few children are totally deaf, but some children will need hearing aids to amplify the sound. Cochlea implants are a kind of hearing aid that send electrical signals to the brain. Radio aids can help you to communicate clearly with the child even if there is background noise. Most of the activities in this book that support children with hearing difficulties are aimed at children who have significant and long-term hearing difficulties and who are therefore on your setting's SEN register.

How you can help

● As an early years practitioner, you are in a good position to identify hearing difficulty early on. Early identification of hearing impairment is vital because it affects language development. So often, a child is failing to hear important sounds just at the stage when they should be developing vocabulary and abstract thinking skills.

● Speak with the parents or carers of the child and with the health visitor if you have any concerns. Most health authorities have specialist

community doctors to assess hearing and, if necessary, they will then refer the child to the specialist Ear, Nose and Throat Consultant.

● If a child is known to have a significant hearing impairment, there is likely to be an advisory support teacher involved. Contact your local service for hearing impaired children through the Local Education Authority or Early Years Partnership.

● Make sure that you have the child's attention before speaking. Stand or stoop so that you can see each other's faces, make eye contact, use their name and keep your words clear and uncluttered.

● Ensure that background noise is kept down by using soft surfaces to absorb sound. It is helpful to have an area into which you can withdraw if you need to be quiet or to work and concentrate in a smaller group.

● Make sure that the areas in your setting are well lit so that you can see faces clearly. If you are sitting in front of a sunny window, your mouth will not be seen.

● Speak clearly and slowly and do not shout. Find out all you can about the child's usual method of communication and link into this.

● Keep up to date with any signs that the child might be using, so that you can use and understand these to clarify speech. Ask the speech and language therapist if you can attend any signing courses that would be helpful. Teach all the children some simple signs to accompany action songs and activities.

● Make a note of unusual words or any words that the child does not understand, so that you can build the correct words into their practical experiences. You will find that many of the activities in this book aim to help children with hearing difficulties by identifying or teaching gaps in abstract vocabulary and concept development.

● Use gesture and expression to make the meaning of what you say clear. Children who are using 'total communication' will be learning how to cue into all the non-verbal clues that you give when you speak and communicate.

● Make sure that you know how to use and adjust any special equipment that the child might have in order to hear more clearly. Ask the parents or carers to give you a demonstration. Remember to remove or switch off a radio aid if you are no longer wishing to communicate with the child. If you are still wearing it in the staff room later, you will be heard clearly!

Making a child feel settled

Welcoming a child with sensory impairment into your setting needs some careful planning and preparation. Find out who is already

involved and gather as much information as you need to know about the child's condition, what it actually means for the child, and what the implications are for you and the setting. If the child has SEN, there is likely to be a specialist teacher for children with hearing or visual impairment already involved from the LEA. Children with significant hearing loss are also usually referred to a speech and language therapist

who might be able to work with you to set and monitor learning targets and opportunities for the child. Make sure that you feel positive and welcoming from the start thanks to the information that you have gathered and to the planning that you have done with the parents or carers and colleagues. There is a list of useful addresses on page 95. The RNIB produces a useful video called *The World in Our Hands* for colleagues to watch before welcoming a child with visual impairment to the setting.

Be assured that you should not have to make major alterations to the structure of your setting or your routine. Most of your toys and activities will be just as suitable for the child with sensory impairment, although you might find that the child plays slightly differently with some of them. For the first few days, consider asking the parents or carers to send in some favourite toys and play things to bridge the gap between home and setting. Set up a few visits before the child starts at your setting, so that they can become familiar with your layout and activities, while still reassured by a parent or carer. This is also an excellent time for you to ask questions and to get to know the child and their particular needs.

Each child, regardless of their special need, will take a different time to settle and relax with you. Consider arranging for an adult to be the key worker so that the child can get to know them better, and so that they can support the child when playing with other children. Children with little or no sight find it hard to cope with too many new people or voices at once, so start with a small group and build up. The RNIB suggests that a home corner can become a secure base for a child with little or no vision. This small and defined space can soon become familiar and feel 'safe' to the child who will gradually welcome in other children and expand their horizons with your support and encouragement. Encourage them to try new experiences and learn familiar routes around the play area. It may be helpful to take children with visual difficulties around the setting to demonstrate what activities you have on offer on a regular basis.

Looking for special opportunities

Children with sensory difficulties may need more repetition of new learning than other children. Look for opportunities to reinforce

learning by practising a new skill or a new word in different situations. It will become easier if you are clear about what it is that you are aiming to teach and why. For example, if you have been working with a child on the concept of 'more', bring this into construction play, sand play, water play, cookery and many other types of activity. The 'Learning objective for all the children' and 'Individual learning target' provided in all the activities in Chapters 3 to 8 will help you with this.

For children with visual impairment, look for opportunities for them to feel and explore by touch whenever possible. For example, when you are cooking, encourage them to handle the ingredients, or when you are telling a story, invite them to feel and explore 'props'. For children with hearing impairment, use whatever means of communication is available to help the child to link word to action and to develop confidence in communicating with others.

Providing the most appropriate learning opportunities within the early years curriculum

Personal, social and emotional development

Children with sensory impairment may need more encouragement than others to 'have a go' at new activities and to build confidence. Those who do 'have a go' and succeed grow in confidence and self-esteem. They are also more likely to try next time. In turn, a child who 'has a go' and fails will quickly lose confidence and self esteem and will be less likely to try next time. Children who cannot hear or see fully lack an important tool for communicating smoothly with other people. They can quickly lose confidence in communicating and playing with other children if they are not supported. You need to act as a 'bridge' and facilitate their early interactions; therefore, the area of Personal, social and emotional development presents particular challenges to you as early years educator.

● Encourage the child to settle in and feel safe with you, then try new activities, one at a time.

● Support the child so that they feel successful.

● Start by playing alongside the child with one other child, then encourage success in a larger group of children.

● Use your running commentary to tell or sign to the child what is happening around them.

● Introduce words to describe textures and feelings.

● Allow the child to take responsibilities for themselves and their own actions whenever the opportunity arises.

● Work from the child's strengths and interests in order to build on confidence.

● Give the child clear information about behaviour, and expect from them the same general behaviour as from other members of the group.

Communication, language and literacy

This area of learning is again particularly challenging to a child who has sensory impairment. Without the usual opportunities to link talking, listening and seeing with actions, these children may take longer than others to develop concepts and reasoning skills. This is not because they are slow thinkers; it is because they have not received the same information through their natural experiences as have their sighted or hearing peers. Be conscious of this and structure the child's experiences to compensate using many of the ideas that have been given previously in this book.

● A child that is blind will find it hard to play imaginatively since small toys or representations do not 'feel' like the real thing, even though they 'look' alike. Use your words to talk through what your small toys are; imaginative play can develop but is likely to be a little later than for others.

● Role-play depends on careful looking at and listening to others, and also pretending. You might need to give the child extra support or prepare them ahead for what you will be doing.

● Encourage turn-taking in conversation at circle time. Always use the children's names when there is a child with visual impairment.

● Enlist a key worker to develop one-to-one conversations. Notice any gaps in language or understanding and plan activities that teach to these gaps.

● Use real objects or practical experiences at story time to hold the child's attention and illustrate the story.

● Provide tactile letters for a child who is visually impaired. Print should be bold and clear, with good contrast.

● Look for a range of multi-sensory or tactile picture books for the children to enjoy together.

● Speak to the specialist teacher for sensory impairment about the particular method of communication and recording to use with the child who needs support.

Mathematical development

Children with sensory impairment may have missed opportunities to develop an understanding of visual quantity, counting or the vocabulary of mathematics such as 'more', 'less' and 'same as'. Look for opportunities to develop the children's mathematical skills using a range

of different senses, and be aware of any apparent gaps in understanding. Children may also have a poor understanding of time sequences and need you to provide concrete examples and experiences of time and what it actually means to us.

● Use real experiences to provide opportunities for counting, such as counting out the beakers at drinks time.

● Look for apparatus that is pleasant to handle as well as to count or recognize, such as an abacus, magnetic number shapes and dice that can be identified by touch.

● Sorting and matching games are ideal. Use the senses that are strong and well developed to support the senses that are weak, for example, by sorting by texture or shape.

● Enjoy number rhymes and action games that encourage counting and the understanding of concepts, such as big and small. Use props if these are helpful.

Knowledge and understanding of the world

Providing real experiences will help children with sensory impairments to compensate for missed opportunities. With your understanding of the child's individual needs, you will be able to plan these. Nature walks can involve touching, feeling, listening and looking, depending on the child's needs. Again, your own language can be used to supply the missing links between words and actions.

● Provide a range of objects to explore and inspect at close range with your commentary and support.

● Show the child how to use tools and implements, using gentle hand-over-hand support if necessary.

● Explain details of changes and patterns to a child who cannot see these. Explain sounds to a child who cannot hear them.

● Use floor and surface textures, sounds and sights to 'map' the play and learning area for a child whose senses are impaired.

Physical development

This Area of Learning is going to be particularly challenging for a child who has little sight, as their confidence could easily be lost. Therefore, most of the activities suggested in Chapter 7 ('Physical development') are targeted at children who have visual impairment.

● Use soft play and ball pools to encourage movement in a small, well-defined area.

● Look for opportunities for the child to move quickly and safely in larger spaces, too.

● Teach the use of echolocation to a child who is blind.

● Consider trying to change the ground surfaces near to boundaries in your setting,

for example, by creating a grassed or paved edge to a play area in your outdoor environment.

● Use physical demonstration or prompting to teach new movements.
● Encourage climbing and be thorough in your use of safety matting and supervision.
● Develop the vocabulary for 'right', 'left', 'forwards' and 'backwards' as soon as you can for a child with visual impairment.
● Use one-to-one supervision where you feel it is necessary for safety, aiming to allow the child the greatest independence possible.

Creative development

Wonderful opportunities for multi-sensory learning are provided in this Area of Learning. Craft materials can be enjoyed as much for their handling as for their appearance, and musical instruments can be enjoyed as much for their feel and appearance as for their sound. Provide a range of materials for handling, feeling and exploring. Use your words to link labels to concepts.

● Allow extra time for the child with sensory impairment to explore the craft materials or instruments before creating with or playing them.
● Bear in mind that role-play and imaginative creations may be more difficult for the child with sensory impairment, particularly visual impairment.
● Remember that children with visual impairment may not connect with the usual facial expressions and non-verbal signals during dance or drama.

The following six chapters provide activity ideas for each of the six Areas of Learning. Use these flexibly, depending on the individual child and your particular circumstances.

PERSONAL, SOCIAL AND EMOTIONAL DEVELOPMENT

Children with sensory difficulties may need your support to make friends and play socially. This chapter includes ideas for meeting and greeting each other, as well as ways of developing confidence.

LEARNING OBJECTIVE FOR ALL THE CHILDREN
● to form good relationships with peers.

INDIVIDUAL LEARNING TARGET
● to locate another child by sound. 👁

Sound beacon

Group size
Eight to 20 children.

What you need
A toy that gives a continuous sound such as a musical box or Lego 'Musical Apple' available from the RNIB toy catalogue (see pages 95 and 96); adult helper.

What to do
The Lego 'Musical Apple' has a little worm inside. If he is pushed in, the apple makes music; if he is pushed in once more, he pops out again.

Sit together in a circle on the floor. Introduce the musical toy and pass it around for each child to look at and feel. Come into the circle and sit in the middle. Place the musical toy beside you so that it is silent, and cover your eyes so that you cannot see. Ask your helper beforehand to creep in and take the toy, then encourage all the children to place their hands behind their backs. The helper should hold the toy behind their back, setting it so that it makes its sound. Uncover your eyes and emphasize moving and listening around the circle until you can hear the sound. Say the name of the person that you think is holding the toy. This person should then lift up their hands to show if you are correct.

Once the children know what to do, invite them to take it in turns to be the 'hider' and the 'seekers'. Help them to remember each other's names, if necessary.

LINKS WITH HOME
Suggest to parents and carers that they play a game in which they hide a musical box or mobile phone with its jingle sounding and encourage their children to find it by listening for the sound.

Special support
If you are working with a child who has a severe visual impairment (so that visual recognition is not possible), play a version of the game in which you tap the knees of the person that you think is holding the toy. That person should then confirm whether or not they have the toy by saying, 'Yes, Sam has the toy' or 'No, Ginny has not got the toy'. This helps the child to match the voice with the name.

Extension
Play a version of the game with different musical instruments.

LEARNING OBJECTIVE FOR ALL THE CHILDREN
● to be confident to try new activities and speak in a familiar group.

INDIVIDUAL LEARNING TARGETS
● to develop touch 👁
● to watch carefully and join in with confidence. 👂

Snake dance

Group size
Eight to 20 children.

What you need
A long, stuffed fabric snake or similar (such as a draught excluder); selection of toys or objects.

What to do
Invent a funny name for the snake and introduce it to the children. Make it have a friendly personality so that it does not become scary to the children.

Sit together in a circle on the floor. Show the children how to gently pass the snake through their hands so that it travels around the circle. As the snake goes around, sing this song to the tune of 'The Farmer's in His Dell' (Traditional).

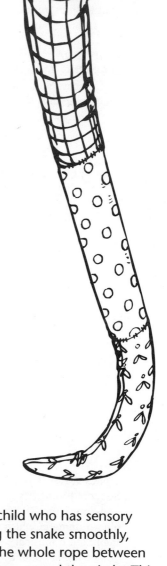

> We pass the snake around,
> We pass the snake around,
> Who's got the head
> As we pass the snake around?
>
> *Hannah Mortimer*

Stop at the end of the verse to see who has got the snake's head. At this point, introduce a simple challenge based on the topic that you are working on at the time, for example, to say their name, to count a simple set of objects in the centre of the circle or to identify a 'big' or 'little' object. Celebrate their success and sing another verse as the snake travels on.

Special support
This activity will be particularly enjoyed by a child who has sensory difficulties. If the child has difficulty in passing the snake smoothly, attach the snake to a circle of rope and pass the whole rope between your hands so that the snake is gradually drawn around the circle. This variation will give everyone something to do.

Extension
Introduce simple challenges after each verse, gradually extending them to encourage the children to think. This activity will allow each child to be challenged at their particular level of ability.

LINKS WITH HOME
Suggest that parents and carers play a simple 'Pass the parcel' game with their children at home, using a big teddy bear that is easy to locate and handle.

How do I feel?

Group size
Four to six children.

What you need
A quiet, well-lit area to sit in, with soft surfaces.

What to do
Sit together in a circle. Explain to the children that you are going to think about how your voice and face help to tell people how you are feeling. Start by saying 'hello' to the children with a happy expression on your face. Ask them to tell you what your face looks like. Go around the circle and encourage the children to take turns to say 'hello' with a happy expression. Repeat for sad faces, then angry faces.

Now ask the children what would happen if you covered your face. How would the children know how you were feeling? Cover your face with your hands and say, in a very sad voice, 'Hello, my name is… and today I am feeling very sad'. Ask the children if they can guess from your tone of voice how your are feeling. Go around the circle and let the children take turns to say what their names are in a sad tone of voice. Repeat for angry voices and happy voices.

Special support
The soft surfaces will absorb sounds and make it easier for the children to hear one another. When working with a child who has hearing impairment, make sure that you have reduced background noise and that it is easy to see and hear each other. Work areas need to be well lit so that your mouth movements and facial expressions will show clearly.

Extension
Introduce new voices and faces, for example, surprised, curious, bored and lazy.

LEARNING OBJECTIVE FOR ALL THE CHILDREN
● to respond to a range of feelings and expressions.

INDIVIDUAL LEARNING TARGET
● to identify sad/happy/cross faces.

LINKS WITH HOME
Ask parents and carers to play 'Guess how I am feeling' with their children.

LEARNING OBJECTIVE FOR ALL THE CHILDREN
● to form good relationships with peers.

INDIVIDUAL LEARNING TARGET
● to play co-operatively with another child. 👁 👂

My den

Group size
Two children, then three or four children.

What you need
A large, clear area; old sheets or bed covers; chairs; large cardboard boxes; large play equipment suitable for constructing a den.

What to do
Place the materials close by and suggest to the child that you are targeting that you could make a den together. Show them different ways in which a simple shelter could be made, and emphasize any safety rules that you feel might be necessary. Encourage the child to design their own den, for example, a picnic area, a bed or an office space. Stay close by to help with any additional props that might be needed such as cups and plates, soft toys and so on.

Once the den is built, ask the child to invite a friend to come to see the den and establish a game to play with them. Then invite one or two children to join them, and look for opportunities to encourage friendly behaviour and to ensure that they have fun together.

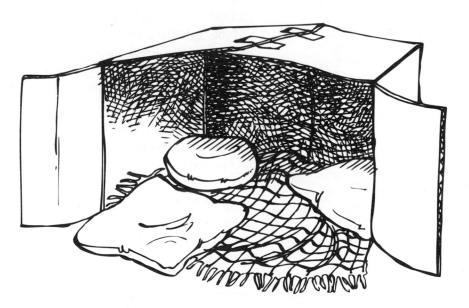

Special support
Children with sensory difficulties sometimes find the initial stages of making friends difficult because other children may 'give up' if they do not receive the usual social signals of chattiness, smiles or shared play. Act as a catalyst to bring the children together and support their play. Encourage the child that you are targeting to play with just one partner, introducing the other children only when the child is ready.

Extension
Older children can design and plan a den before they build it. Encourage them to select the equipment as they need it and to experiment with different constructions.

LINKS WITH HOME
Suggest to parents and carers that they use the backs of armchairs and an old cover to make an excellent den at home.

LEARNING OBJECTIVE FOR ALL THE CHILDREN
● to work harmoniously as part of a group.

INDIVIDUAL LEARNING TARGET
● to locate the position of an object by sound. 👁

Gentle jingle

Group size
Eight to 20 children.

What you need
A ring of jingle bells; tambourine; shakers.

What to do
Sit together in a circle on the floor. Introduce the jingle bells and make a loud noise with them. Pass them around the circle and invite each child in turn to make a loud noise. When the bells come back to you, show the children how to pass them very gently so that this time they make no sound at all. Pass the bells around the circle as quietly as possible.

Now introduce the tambourine and take turns to make a loud noise with it as it is passed around the circle. When you try passing it silently, invite a child to stand in the centre with their hands covering their eyes. Can they turn towards the sound? If there is no sound being made at all, praise the children for handling the instruments very gently.

Finally, pass the shaker around the circle, first noisily, then silently. Invite the children to take turns to stand in the middle and turn towards the sound.

Special support
Encourage the child with visual difficulties to locate the sound and turn or point towards it. If there is a child with hearing impairment, establish the instruments that they can hear and use these for an adapted version of the game. Pass the instrument silently around the circle and occasionally point to a child who has the instrument to indicate that they should make a noise with it. Invite the child with the hearing difficulty to stand in the middle with their eyes covered and to turn towards the sound as soon as they hear it.

Extension
Challenge the children to pass several instruments silently around the circle at once, perhaps in opposite directions.

LINKS WITH HOME
Explain to parents and carers that you have been thinking about loud and quiet sounds. Suggest to them that they encourage quiet indoor voices at home if their children get too noisy.

LEARNING OBJECTIVES FOR ALL THE CHILDREN
● to respond to significant experiences
● to have a developing respect for their own lives and for others.

INDIVIDUAL LEARNING TARGET
● to be confident to speak in the group.
👁 👂

LINKS WITH HOME
Invite parents and carers to help you to prepare for this activity. Explain that you would like the children to feel confident in sharing a piece of news from home. Ask them to let their children bring in a holiday souvenir, favourite toy, photograph or something interesting that they have found. Remind them to put the child's name on it.

Shared news

Group size
Four to ten children.

What you need
Something brought in from home by each child to talk about and share; teddy bear.

What to do
As the children arrive at your setting, invite them to put their special things that they have brought from home on one side ready to share at news time. Be aware of any children who have not brought anything so that you can help them to choose something that they like from your setting to talk about.

Sit together in a circle on the floor. Introduce the teddy bear, and ask the children to pass it around the circle as you chant, 'Pass the bear around, pass the bear around, pass the bear around and… STOP!'. Let the bear stop at a different child each time and encourage the child to 'show and tell' while the others listen. Help each child to talk about the object that they have chosen to share by asking questions such as, 'Why did you choose this?', 'What do you like about it?' and so on. Ask the other children if they have any questions that they would like to ask.

If appropriate, encourage the child to pass their own object around the circle. Then sing the bear song again until it stops at a new child. Continue until everyone who wants to has had a turn.

Special support
Children with sensory difficulties sometimes find it hard to share experiences unless they have something concrete to talk about. This activity can be a good way of encouraging them to speak confidently about something that they are really interested in.

Extension
Encourage the children to draw a picture of their favourite object and to write a sentence about it.

LEARNING OBJECTIVE FOR ALL THE CHILDREN
● to understand that there need to be codes of gentleness.

INDIVIDUAL LEARNING TARGET
● to become familiar with their friends using gentle touch.
◉

Close encounters

Group size
Six to 12 children.

What you need
A carpeted area to sit on; loose soft scarf; adult helper.

What to do
Sit together in a circle on the floor. Sing this song to the tune of 'Here We Go Round the Mulberry Bush' (Traditional).

> This is the way we say hello, say hello, say hello,
> This is the way we say hello, on a cold and frosty morning.
> Who will we meet to say hello, say hello, say hello?
> Who will we meet to say hello, on a cold and frosty morning?
>
> *Hannah Mortimer*

Begin by taking the first turn in this guessing game yourself. Move to the centre of the circle and tie the scarf loosely around your eyes. Your helper should then signal to one of the children and lead them to meet you in the centre. They should reassure the child as you gently feel the child's face, shoulders and hair, and guess who is in front of you. Encourage the other children not to call out who the child is! Once you have guessed correctly, remove your scarf and sing together, for example:

Mrs Kahn and Peter will say hello, say hello, say hello!
Mrs Kahn and Peter will say hello, on a cold and frosty morning!

Repeat with the children taking turns at wearing the scarf and guessing whom the person who joins them is. Praise the children for being gentle.

Special support
Support the child with sensory impairment in the same way as the others. Be aware that the child with severe hearing impairment may feel particularly isolated if they are blindfolded, so offer a choice.

Extension
Play 'Guess the feet' with the children. Lead a child into the centre of the circle with a cover over their top half and encourage the other children to guess who it is, perhaps from the colour of their shoes.

LINKS WITH HOME
Explain to parents and carers that you have been talking about being gentle. Ask them to encourage their children to stroke their pets gently or cuddle a baby gently.

LEARNING OBJECTIVE FOR ALL THE CHILDREN
● to maintain attention, concentrate and sit quietly when appropriate.

INDIVIDUAL LEARNING TARGET
● to beat their name. 👁 👂

Good vibrations

Group size
Six to 16 children.

What you need
A large tambour or flat drum and a beater.

What to do
Sit together in a circle and show the children the instrument. Pass the beater around the circle and invite each child to take a turn to make a loud sound while you hold the drum. Repeat, asking each child to make a quiet sound.

Now, in turn, give each child a simple rhythm to copy, perhaps two loud beats, three quiet ones or a rapid succession of beats. Then give each child another rhythm to copy, but this time add words to help their memory, for example, 'chips', 'wa-ter', 'saus-a-ges', 'ba-na-na', 'hap-py birth-day' and so on. Encourage the child that is imitating you to repeat the word as they beat the rhythm. Lift the drum away swiftly as they finish to prevent them from adding extra drumbeats at the end. This will help to ensure success.

Finally, move around the circle, inviting each child in turn to say and beat the syllables of their name, for example, 'Ner-gis', 'Cal-lum', 'Jack' and so on.

Special support
Invite the child with severe hearing impairment to lay a hand lightly on the drum surface so that they can sense the vibrations. Encourage the child with severe visual impairment to feel where the drum is before beating it.

Extension
Older children with hearing impairment might like to feel the vibrations of all the children's names by holding the drum with you.

LINKS WITH HOME
Ask parents and carers to help their children to clap the syllables of their names at home.

LEARNING OBJECTIVE FOR ALL THE CHILDREN
● to understand that people have different needs.

INDIVIDUAL LEARNING TARGET
● to practise signing.

I like you!

Group size
Six to 12 children.

What you need
A large floor area.

What to do
Stand together in a circle. Spread out your arms so that you are standing fairly wide apart. Now drop hands and sit down. Talk to the children about what it means to be 'friends' and to behave in a 'friendly' way. Ask them for ideas. Now teach them this song to the tune of 'This Old Man' (Traditional).

> I like you, you like me,
> We're as happy as can be!
> I like you and you like me
> What a friendly company!
>
> *Hannah Mortimer*

I	Like	You
Me		

Teach the children the Makaton signs for 'I like you' and for 'You like me' (see above).

Repeat the song and add the signs in the first and third lines. Ask the children to stay sitting down as you sing to them. Move to the child that you are targeting, and sing and sign the song to them. Now ask the child to stand up and help you to decide which child to move to next. Stand together in front of the new child and both sing and sign the song to them. At the end of the verse, the first child should sit down, and the new child should join you and help to decide who to move to next. As the game progresses, always ask the last child who has joined you to choose the next child to sing and sign to. Continue until everyone who wants to has had a turn.

Special support
Make simple signing a regular part of your session.

Extension
Introduce some more signs for key words within the verse, for example, 'happy' or 'friendly'.

LINKS WITH HOME
Talk with the support teacher or the parents or carers of the child that you are targeting about any signs that the child is using regularly.

PERSONAL, SOCIAL & EMOTIONAL DEVELOPMENT

LEARNING OBJECTIVES FOR ALL THE CHILDREN
● to work as part of a group
● to form good relationships.

INDIVIDUAL LEARNING TARGET
● to locate a friend by sound. 👁

Meeting up

Group size
Three or four children.

What you need
Musical badges, each playing a different tune; large teddy bear.

What to do
Collect musical badges from various greetings cards so that you have a collection of different tunes. Pin all the badges on to a large teddy bear. Gather the children together and show them the badges. Invite each child to press each badge in turn and let them choose one to wear for the activity. Pin the badges carefully on to the children. Warn them not to remove the badges without your help so that you can make sure that the pins do not prick them.

   Now sit together on the floor. Take it in turns to play your badges while everyone else listens carefully. Invite all the children to cover their eyes with their hands, then tap one child gently and signal for them to play their badge. Encourage the other children to keep their eyes covered as they guess whose badge is playing. Then say, 'Open your eyes now! Let's see if you were right!'. Play the badge again and celebrate success. Repeat this several times.

Special support
Ask an adult helper to wear a musical badge and press it when they are playing near a child with visual impairment to announce their presence. Wearing an individual scent can be helpful, too. The helper should also announce themselves by name, for example, 'Hello *(child's name)*. It's *(their name)* here. Can I play too?'.

Extension
Give each child their own percussion instrument to play instead of wearing the badges.

LINKS WITH HOME
Ask parents and carers to play a game to encourage their children to hide their eyes, listen to sounds and say what they are.

COMMUNICATION, LANGUAGE AND LITERACY

This chapter encourages progress in communication, language and literacy. This is a key area for children with sensory difficulties and these skills often take longer to acquire.

LEARNING OBJECTIVES FOR ALL THE CHILDREN
● to enjoy listening to spoken language
● to listen with enjoyment and respond to stories.

INDIVIDUAL LEARNING TARGET
● to concentrate and follow a simple story ◉ ♪

LINKS WITH HOME
Invite parents and carers to send in favourite stories so that they can be set on to acetate.

Story projections

Group size
Six to eight children.

What you need
The photocopiable sheet on page 86; A3 paper; sheet of black card; overhead projector and screen; pencil; scissors; tracing paper; coloured acetate sheets; washable coloured projector pens.

What to do
Copy the photocopiable sheet on to A3 paper. Trace the characters on to a sheet of black card, then cut out the shadow puppets carefully. Familiarize yourself with the story of *Jack and the Beanstalk* (*First Favourite Tales* series, Ladybird Books) so that you can tell it to the children from

memory. Set up the overhead projector and screen where they will not get knocked, where you can darken the area and where there are not too many distractions.

Gather the children together and begin to tell your story as you place the shadow puppets on to the projector plate. Use the projector pens to draw in any background scenery that you need, such as Jack's house, the road, the beanstalk and so on. Invite the children to suggest what you should draw.

After you have finished telling the story, encourage the children to re-enact it with your support, using the shadow puppets and the projector.

Special support
If you are working with a child who has visual difficulties, spend a little individual time before the activity experimenting with different-coloured acetates for the background colour. Find out which colours help the child to see the shadow puppets best and which coloured pens are easiest to see.

Extension
Use washable projector pens to draw pictures on acetate sheets for the scenery, or invent new stories to illustrate with shadow puppets.

Odds and ends

Group size
Six to 12 children.

What you need
A selection of natural objects such as a sea shell, piece of bark, smooth stone, fir cone, lump of coral, feather and so on; 'precious' box with a lid, approximately 10cm³; large cardboard box with a lid.

What to do
Hide the natural objects in the large cardboard box and put these to one side of you. Place one of the objects inside the precious box and close its lid.

Invite the children to sit in a circle on the floor. Tell them that inside your special box there is something that you are going to describe to them. Lift the lid and peep inside. Begin to tell the children what you can see, for example, 'It is pink and has lots of little branches'. Touch the object and tell the children what you can feel, for example, 'It feels rough and a bit sharp'. Pass the box around the circle so that each child can look at and feel the object. As you talk, emphasize the key words, for example, 'Can you *feel* how rough it is?' and 'What does it *look* like?'. When everyone has had a turn, lift the object out and tell the children what it is called and where you would find it, for example, 'This is called coral and you can find it underneath the sea'.

Place a new object in the box and ask a child to describe it to the others. Use your previous questions to help them, for example, 'What does it *look* like?' and 'Does it feel *rough* or *smooth*?'. Remember that the focus of this activity is to organize talk when describing, not necessarily to guess what is in the box.

Special support
Children with sensory impairments will need more practice than others in linking actions to words. Use this activity as an opportunity to attach words to sensations by encouraging the child to describe what they can feel, see or hear.

Extension
Invite the children to play a guessing game with the natural objects and the descriptions.

LEARNING OBJECTIVE FOR ALL THE CHILDREN
● to use talk to sequence thinking and ideas.

INDIVIDUAL LEARNING TARGET
● to enjoy and talk about a sensory/tactile picture book. 👁 👂

Scratch and sniff

Group size
Three or four children at a time.

What you need
An adult helper; local library; magazines; scissors; glue; old picture book or scrapbook.

What to do
Arrange a visit to your local library to visit the children's section. Alternatively, contact your local school's library service and ask them to lend you a selection of tactile and multi-sensory picture books, for example, books with interesting textures, flaps to lift or cords to pull, moving parts, 'scratch and sniff' pages and books that produce sounds. Invite the children to help you to choose some books that are interesting to feel, smell or listen to as well as to look at. Display the books in a comfortable corner and ask an adult helper to be constantly there to share the books with the children.

Finally, prepare your own 'scratch and sniff' book. Adapt an old picture book, or cut out pictures and glue them into a scrapbook, and add a simple text. Cut out 'scratch and sniff' patches from glossy magazines and glue these into position on top of existing pictures. Invite the children to scratch the patch and ask them if they can smell the perfume.

LINKS WITH HOME
Ask parents and carers to lend you any books that they have found fun to handle. Build up and share a book list of useful selections from the local library or bookshop.

Special support
Children with sensory impairment enjoy books that allow them to explore stories and words with more than one sense. Try to have a good selection of multi-sensory and tactile books in your book corner.

Extension
Let the children make their own books using magazine advertisements.

LEARNING OBJECTIVES FOR ALL THE CHILDREN
● to hear and say initial sounds in names
● to use their phonic knowledge to identify names.

INDIVIDUAL LEARNING TARGET
● to become familiar with finger-spelling. 👂

I spy my friend

Group size
Three or four children.

What you need
The finger-spelling alphabet on the photocopiable sheet on page 87.

What to do
Familiarize yourself with the finger-spelling alphabet on the photocopiable sheet. Gather the children together and help each child to identify the first sound of their name. Spend a few minutes thinking of other words that begin with the same sound. Now teach each child how to finger-spell the first sound of their name.

When the children are ready, play a game of 'I spy'. Start with 'I spy with my little eye, someone beginning with... *(first sound of a child's name)*'. As you say the sound, make the finger-spelling, too. Play this a few times as the children become used to hearing the first sound of their names. Then try the activity again with just the finger-spellings. Add the first sound of the name if you need to as an extra clue.

LINKS WITH HOME
Give parents and carers a copy of the photocopiable sheet on page xx but make sure that it fits in with the child's communication plan. Sometimes, signing is delayed in order to encourage a child to make maximum use of their residual hearing.

Special support
Ask the sensory support teacher whether it would be useful to introduce finger-spelling to a child with severe hearing impairment as part of your early phonic work. You may be able to teach a child how to finger-spell their name. Some children who have multi-sensory impairment (those who cannot see or hear) use a version of finger-spelling in which the 'speaker' makes the shapes on the child's hand.

Extension
Play 'I spy with my little eye, someone who ends with... *(last sound of a child's name)*'.

LEARNING OBJECTIVES FOR ALL THE CHILDREN
● to know that print carries meaning
● to read their names.

INDIVIDUAL LEARNING TARGET
● to identify their name by touch. 👁

Touch cards

Group size
Three or four children at a time.

What you need
Rough sandpaper; scissors; glue; card; pen; templates for forming large letters, approximately 10cm high.

Preparation
Mark out and cut out the letters of each child's name from sandpaper, aiming for letters of approximately 10cm high. Place these safely to one side. Now cut out lengths of card large enough for the children to mount the letters of their names on.

What to do
Invite the children to join you. Show each child in turn the letters of their name. Sound the letters out as you handle them and encourage the child to identify the first letter of their name. Help them to sequence the letters to form their name, and support them as they glue the letters on to the cards to make a tactile name card. Encourage the children to feel each letter and to say the sound, or to scan the whole word with their fingers, saying their name.

Special support
Children with severe visual impairment can use the tactile cards to identify their work, their tray and so on. Make little tactile shapes to identify possessions, for example, a sandpaper snail to represent a child's coat peg.

Extension
Use individual, tactile letter cards to make up simple words, and encourage the children to touch them to guess the words.

LINKS WITH HOME
Send home individual, tactile letter cards consisting of all the letters in the children's names. Ask parents and carers to help their children to arrange the letters in the correct order and also to play a guessing game using touch to identify the first letters of their names.

Going on holiday

Group size
Six to 12 children.

What you need
A quiet area to sit in; selection of musical instruments.

What to do
Gather the children together for a story. Say that you think that it would be a good idea for you all to go on a pretend holiday together. Ask the children questions such as, 'Where should we go?', 'How will we travel there?', 'What do we need to pack?', 'Where will we stay?', 'What will we do when we get there?', 'What will we eat?' and so on. Use the questions and answers to help the children to decide on the detail of your story.

Act out the story in sections and have sound effects to accompany your role-play. Choose an instrument that makes a good 'chuff-chuff' sound for the train, make engine noises with your lips for a car, or strap yourselves in carefully for take-off in an aeroplane. Again, use the children's own ideas for sound effects and role-play. Use rainmakers for gentle sandy-beach sounds and coconut shells for a seaside donkey's 'clip-clop'.

When you have finished the story, and have all returned home, try to re-enact the main features, remembering the sequences and the sound effects that you chose.

Special support
Role-play depends on a true understanding of real life situations and may be more difficult for a child with sensory impairment. Plan this carefully by talking with these children first. They will then be able to contribute some ideas of their own.

Extension
Invite the children to draw and write postcards to send home from your holiday destination.

LEARNING OBJECTIVE FOR ALL THE CHILDREN
● to retell narratives in the correct sequence.

INDIVIDUAL LEARNING TARGETS
● to retell part of a story 👁 👂
● to add a sound effect to a simple story. 👁

LINKS WITH HOME
Invite parents and carers to send in props, souvenirs or snapshots of recent holidays to prompt the children's ideas.

LEARNING OBJECTIVE FOR ALL THE CHILDREN
● to extend their vocabulary.

INDIVIDUAL LEARNING TARGET
● to point to named body parts. 👁

The nose song

Group size
Six to 24 children.

What you need
A carpeted area to sit on.

What to do
Gather the children together and sit on the floor. Introduce this song, singing very slowly and encouraging the children to do the actions at the same time. Sing it to the tune of 'Here We Go Round the Mulberry Bush' (Traditional).

> Wiggle your nose and clap your hands,
> Wiggle your nose and clap your hands,
> Wiggle your nose and clap your hands,
> We can do it faster!

Repeat the song at a rapid pace and have fun as you try to keep up with the actions. When you reach the last line, substitute 'Now let's choose another!'.

Ask the children to think of two more actions and body parts to build into your song. Start again with your new sequence, for example, 'Pat your head and tap your toes' or 'Touch your ears and wiggle your tongue'. Each time, start very slowly, emphasizing the key words of the body parts and the actions. Then repeat it quickly and share the fun. Try to carry out the children's own ideas so long as these are sensible.

Special support
If the child that you are targeting is just beginning to learn body parts, keep this song very simple. Sit beside the child and touch their nose, ears, toes and so on as you sing the words to them.

Extension
Build up to a sequence of three or four body parts and actions, for example, 'Wiggle your nose, tap your ears, tickle your tummy and click your fingers'.

LINKS WITH HOME
Ask parents and carers to teach their children to point to named body parts at home using their favourite teddies or cuddly toys.

LEARNING OBJECTIVE FOR ALL THE CHILDREN
● to link initial sounds to familiar objects.

INDIVIDUAL LEARNING TARGET
● to identify by touch. 👁 👂

LINKS WITH HOME
Ask parents and carers to help their children by introducing the simpler and more familiar 'I spy' game at home. This is easiest if parents use a small selection of familiar objects that the children can see in front of them.

Touch and feel

Group size
Two children at a time.

What you need
Two identical small plastic animals such as dogs; two bricks; two pencils; two spoons; two small cars; two shoeboxes; pieces of dark cloth to cover the objects; table.

What to do
Arrange one set of objects in each shoebox and cover the tops with the cloths so that the objects cannot be seen. Invite the children to join you to sit at a table. Give each child one of the boxes. Show the children how they can reach underneath the cloth to feel the toys without looking at them. If they are unsure, let them take a quick look first.

Now introduce the game 'I feel' and say, 'I feel with my little fingers something beginning with… "d"' (or 'b', 'p', 's' or 'c'). Initially, this may be difficult for the children, so use trial and error to withdraw different objects, sounding out the initial sound until they find the correct one. Replace the objects and let the children have another turn. They will soon be able to use touch to identify the object and link it to its sound through some very clever 'multi-sensory thinking'.

Special support
Let children with visual impairment be fully involved. Allow them time to feel and identify each object before you begin to play the game.

Extension
Build up the number of objects to be identified. Allow the children to set each other challenges and to play this game without your support.

COMMUNICATION, LANGUAGE & LITERACY

LEARNING OBJECTIVE FOR ALL THE CHILDREN
● to speak clearly and audibly with confidence and control.

INDIVIDUAL LEARNING TARGETS
● to identify a speaker from their voice 👁
● to speak with confidence. 👂

Friendly voices

Group size
One child at a time, then a group of six to 12 children.

What you need
A tape recorder; blank tape.

What to do
Take one child at a time to a quiet area. Explain that you would like them to say something into the tape recorder for the other children to try to guess whose voice it is. Build on the child's own ideas, for example, 'I have long hair, I have brown eyes, I like red, my favourite toy is the slide and I live next door'. Practise this once or twice, then make a recording. Play it back to the child and enjoy the effect that this has! Make sure that the child is happy with the recording and add to it if they want to.

Later, gather a larger group of children together for a listening-and-guessing game. Play the tape back, pausing between each child's voice. Invite the children to guess who is speaking. Why do they think that? Encourage the child whose name has been suggested to say a few words. Were the children correct – is that the same voice?

Special support
Use this as an opportunity to teach any blind child the names of the children who accompany their voice recordings.

Extension
Let older children play other listening-and-guessing games by recording on to tape, for example, descriptions of familiar objects or activities for the listeners to guess.

LINKS WITH HOME
Encourage the friends of a blind child, together with their parents or carers, to make a point of saying 'goodbye' at home time, so that the blind child knows who has left and who is still there.

COMMUNICATION, LANGUAGE & LITERACY

LEARNING OBJECTIVE FOR ALL THE CHILDREN
● to use talk to sequence events.

INDIVIDUAL LEARNING TARGET
● to arrange pictures of a familiar story in order. 👁 👂

Cartoon clips

Group size
Two children at a time.

What you need
The photocopiable sheet on page 88; glue; scissors; card; felt-tipped pens; table.

Preparation
Copy the photocopiable sheet on to card and cut it into four sections. Prepare several blank cards.

What to do
Invite the children to sit with you at a table and spread the cards out in random order. Ask the children if they can tell you what is happening in the pictures. Talk together as the children try to arrange the cards in order, from left to right. Ask, 'What happens first?', 'Then what happens?', 'What happens next?' and 'What happens last?'. Then invite the children to tell you what they think will happen when the elephants stop for their picnic. Finally, ask the children to recount the whole story, using the picture sequence as a clue.

Assist the children as they make up their own story sequences. Use simple illustrations to support their story, then challenge them to arrange these in the correct order.

Special support
If the child that you are targeting has sensory impairment, they might find it easier to build their story on real objects and happenings from their own experiences such as a holiday, what happened at the weekend, when the dog broke the fence and so on.

Extension
Cut out cartoon clips from old comics. Stick them on to card and challenge the children to play a picture sequencing game with them.

LINKS WITH HOME
Ask parents and carers to encourage their children to talk about what happened before a particular event and what will happen next.

MATHEMATICAL DEVELOPMENT

In this chapter, you will find activities for encouraging mathematical development for all the children. There are ideas for teaching early counting and number recognition, position and shape words, as well as early sorting and matching skills.

Feeling big

LEARNING OBJECTIVE FOR ALL THE CHILDREN
● to use language such as 'bigger' and 'smaller'.

INDIVIDUAL LEARNING TARGET
● to identify 'the big one' by feel. 👁

Group size
Four to eight children.

What you need
A drawstring bag; big and small ball; big and small car; big and small brick; big and small teddy bear; other items in pairs, identical except in size.

What to do
Place the objects to one side. Ask the children to sit around you as you place two matching objects into the bag. Talk about them as the children watch you, for example, 'I have a really big ball here (pause to show the children) and this one feels just the same except that it is small' (pause again to emphasize the key word). Now challenge the children in turn to put their hands into the bag and pick out the big ball or the small ball. Do this for the different pairs of objects. Emphasize the key words again as the child shows you what they have picked out, for example, 'Yes – there's the big ball!' and so on. Start to mix and match the objects, for example, 'Can you find me the big car?', 'Can you find me the small brick?', 'Can you find me two big things?' and so on.

Special support
Let children with visual impairment help you to place the objects into the drawstring bag so that they can feel the big ball and the small ball in turn as you talk about their sizes. They will then find it easier to identify them by touch.

Extension
Provide the children with pairs of objects where the size difference is less obvious. Introduce a 'middle-sized' object for the children to feel for as well.

LINKS WITH HOME
Suggest that parents and carers ask their children to find big and small sizes of the same thing, such as a big sock and a small sock, a big slipper and a small slipper, and so on. Who do they belong to?

MATHEMATICAL DEVELOPMENT • MATHEMATICAL DEVELOPMENT • MATHEMATICAL DEVELOPMENT

LEARNING OBJECTIVE FOR ALL THE CHILDREN
● to use language such as 'circle', 'square' and 'triangle'.

INDIVIDUAL LEARNING TARGET
● to identify a circle, square and triangle when asked.

Fishing for shapes

Group size
Three to six children at a time.

What you need
The photocopiable sheet on page 89; A4 sheets of cardboard; felt-tipped pens; scissors; glue; paper clips; large chubby pencils or 20cm lengths of dowelling; string; craft knife (adult use); small horseshoe magnets; table.

Preparation
Create fishing lines by making a small groove with the craft knife approximately 1cm from the blunt end of the chubby pencil or length of dowelling. Use the groove to wrap one end of a piece of string approximately 30cm long. Tie the string securely, then tie a small horseshoe magnet to the other end of the piece of string.

What to do
Invite the children to join you around a table. Give each child a copy of the photocopiable sheet. Talk about the shapes together as you colour them in with the felt-tipped pens. Then support the children as they glue their sheets on to the pieces of cardboard. When the shapes have dried, cut them out. If the card is not too thick, the children might be able to do this themselves. Then show them how to fix a paper clip on to the edge of each shape.

Spread the shapes out on the floor and invite the children to 'fish' for shapes, dangling the magnet until it attracts one of the paper clips attached to a shape. Challenge them to fish for a named shape such as a star or rectangle. If the children are unsure, show them another shape that is the same. Use the game as a natural opportunity to name and identify different shapes.

Special support
Start with a small selection of shapes such as a circle, triangle and square. Then build up the number of shapes. For children with visual impairment, play a feeling version of this game by giving the child one shape and naming it, then challenging them to pick up and feel for another shape just the same.

Extension
Make sandpaper shapes to mount on the wall and invite the children to identify them by touch.

LINKS WITH HOME
Ask parents and carers to help their children to find objects around the house that are shapes like a circle or square.

LEARNING OBJECTIVES FOR ALL THE CHILDREN
● to say and use number names in familiar contexts
● to begin to use the vocabulary associated with adding and subtracting.

INDIVIDUAL LEARNING TARGETS
● to count up to six 👁 👂
● to develop one-to-one correspondence when counting. 👁

Ropes and trees

Group size
Two or three children.

What you need
The photocopiable sheet on page 90; sheet of A3 card; coloured felt-tipped pens or crayons; small plastic jungle animals; large single dice (with well-indented spots); plastic cup.

What to do
This game is a jungle version of 'Snakes and ladders' to play with dice and plastic animals. Copy the photocopiable sheet on to A3 card.

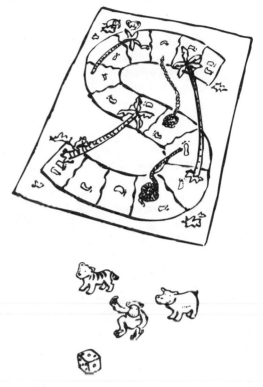

Invite the children to sit at a table with you and show them the board game. Suggest that it would look even better if it were coloured. Encourage the children to talk with you about the jungle scene as you all add colours. When you feel that the board is ready, encourage the children to find four jungle animals to use from a selection of small plastic jungle animals. Show them the dice and spend a little time pointing to and counting the spots.

Now place the chosen jungle animals on the first square, put the dice into the cup and invite the children to take turns to throw the dice. Encourage each child to count the spots on the dice. Use hand-over-hand support if necessary to help them to move each animal in turn that number of squares. If they land on a rope at the end of the count, they should slide down their animal to the square at the bottom of the rope. If they land on a tree, they should make it climb to the top! Make sure that the animals take turns, though it will be different children moving them each time, so no child will lose! The animal that wins is the first one to reach the last square.

Special support
Invite the children to count out loud as the animals move square by square. Encourage children with visual impairment to feel for and count the spots.

Extension
Let older children play complete 'Snakes and ladders' games.

LINKS WITH HOME
Give each child an A3 copy of the photocopiable sheet to take home. Explain to parents and carers how to play the game and ask them to encourage their children to colour in the sheet and play the game with them.

LEARNING OBJECTIVE FOR ALL THE CHILDREN
● to count reliably up to four everyday objects.

INDIVIDUAL LEARNING TARGETS
● to count reliably by touch 👁
● to match colour and sets. 👂

Colour hunt

Group size
Three or four children at a time.

What you need
Sets of brightly coloured and matching objects, for example, a plastic teaset with four red, blue, green and yellow cups, plates, saucers, spoons, forks and knives.

What to do
Spread your objects around so that they are not immediately obvious and the children have to search for them – for example, place them in the home corner, hiding some of it in the cupboards and washing-up bowls.

Gather the children around you and tell them that they are going to play a number game. Give each child a challenge to find you a given number of objects, perhaps a yellow plate. Give each child an individual challenge, for example, 'Can you find me four red plates?', 'Can you find me two yellow cups?' and so on. Continue until you have made up the complete tea set, then role-play a picnic.

Special support
Make sure that the objects are close at hand for a child with visual impairment so that they can feel for them. Use a well-lit area so that the objects can be easily seen if the child has limited vision. This is a useful activity for introducing the signs for different colours if a child with hearing impairment is learning sign language.

Red
(lips)

Blue
(veins)

Green
(grass)

Yellow
(letter Y)

LINKS WITH HOME
Lend colour-matching toys to parents and carers so that they can help their children to learn colour-matching at home.

Extension
Make the challenges more difficult for older children, for example, 'Can you see six things around the room that look like circles?' or 'We have a book shaped like a triangle – can you find it?'.

LEARNING OBJECTIVE FOR ALL THE CHILDREN
● to say and use number names backwards.

INDIVIDUAL LEARNING TARGET
● to join in a simple number rhyme.
👁 👂

Five, four, three, two, one!

Group size
Six to 30 children.

What you need
Five number cards, approximately A4 size, with the numerals 1, 2, 3, 4 and 5 written on.

What to do
Sit down in a circle together. Teach the children this chant.

> Rockets shooting into space, 5, 4, 3, 2, 1 and zero!
> Blast of fire and up we go, 5, 4, 3, 2, 1 and zero!
> Reaching to the highest place, 5, 4, 3, 2, 1 and zero!
> See the tiny earth down below, 5, 4, 3, 2, 1 and zero!
>
> *Hannah Mortimer*

Chant it slowly, then on the refrain place your hands together like a rocket and shoot them high above your heads.

Invite five children to stand in the circle and give them each a number card to hold up. Give the numbers out in a jumbled order. Now invite another child to come and move the children around until they are standing in the correct order – 5, 4, 3, 2, 1. Chant the rhyme again, then invite a new set of children to hold the cards.

Play a different version of this action rhyme by inviting all the children in the circle to hold up five fingers and fold them into their hands, one at a time, as you slowly count 'five', 'four', 'three', 'two', 'one', until they have a clenched fist that they can shoot into the air for 'zero'.

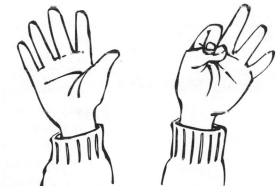

Special support
Use gentle hand-over-hand support to prompt the action for a blind child.

Extension
Challenge older children to count backwards from ten or, perhaps, 20.

LINKS WITH HOME
Ask parents and carers to hold their children's hands and practise counting backwards from five or 20 as they take steps along the pavement together.

Sand search

Group size
Three or four children.

What you need
A selection of six small plastic animals, toys and vehicles; sand tray.

What to do
Ask the children to help you to carry the toys to the sand tray, and play with them for a while so that you know which toys are there. After a while, suggest to the children that they bury all the toys in the sand. Tell them that you are going to search for them. Encourage them to watch and guess as you identify something beneath the sand, for example, 'It's small, it's got wheels on, there's a ladder on the top. It's the… *(fire engine)*'.

Now invite each child to take a turn and use describing words to explain what they can feel. If they are at a loss for words, ask them questions such as, 'Does it have legs or wheels?', 'Does it have a handle?' and so on.

Finally, set the children a challenge to do together, for example, 'Find me all the animals', 'Find me the large car', 'Find me the small bucket' and so on. Introduce positional words into your challenges, for example, 'Can you find another toy underneath that one?' or 'Can you cover the car over with sand?'.

Special support
Make sure that the children with visual impairment have the opportunity to handle and feel all the toys and to hear their names before they are hidden.

Extension
Encourage older children to set challenges to the rest of the group using clever descriptions to help them in their searching and feeling.

LINKS WITH HOME
Suggest to parents and carers that they play a game with their children at bedtime. Ask them to hide one of their child's favourite cuddly toys under the bed covers. Can their child feel beneath the covers and identify the toy by touch?

LEARNING OBJECTIVE FOR ALL THE CHILDREN
● to count reliably up to ten.

INDIVIDUAL LEARNING TARGETS
● to count and imitate hand claps 👁
● to practise using echo to define spaces. 👁

Clapping echo

Group size
Six to 12 children.

What you need
A large place indoors or outdoors that echoes.

What to do
Take the children into the area and stand in a circle. Ask them if they know what an echo is. Call out loudly using a sing-song 'Ec-ho!'. (Imitate the two notes of the 'cuc-koo' to achieve the correct notes.) Now take it in turns to shout, 'Ec-ho!' in the space and listen to the echo returning.

Tell the children that you are going to play an echo game. Explain that you are going to give each child a number of claps and you would like them to repeat them to you. Stand in front of each child in turn, clapping your hands as you count anywhere from one to ten, depending on each child's ability. Encourage the child by counting with them, if necessary, as they repeat the claps back to you. Move to another child, crossing the circle so that your movements are not predictable.

Finish by moving around the space calling out your echoes and listening to how they change as you approach hard surfaces.

Special support
A blind child will have subconsciously been using echolocation since babyhood. However, as you carry out the activity, consciously talk and think about it or else the skill will not develop fully. In fact, many blind children make their own little noises as they move to help this skill.

Extension
Encourage the children to notice how quickly their echo returns to them. Let them try chanting it at different distances from a wall.

LINKS WITH HOME
Encourage the parents or carers of a child who is severely visually impaired to help their child to develop a sense of echo near to hard surfaces. This is a helpful way of learning where you are in space.

Find the musical box

Group size
Four to six children.

What you need
A clockwork musical box.

What to do
Gather the children and show them the musical box. Demonstrate what happens when you wind it up or open the lid. Enjoy the tune together.

Now tell the children that you are going to hide the musical box. Invite a child to be the seeker and ask them to turn away or cover their eyes. Place the musical box somewhere where it cannot easily be seen and let the other children watch you hide it. Place it somewhere that can be easily described such as behind the bricks, underneath the table-cloth or inside the toy-box. Wind it up or open the lid so that it begins to play. Now challenge the children to be really quiet while the seeker begins to listen for the sound. This may be hard for young children, so invite the other children to give spoken clues by describing where to look.

Let the seeker be the next person to hide the musical box with your help. Invite another child to be the next seeker. Continue until each child has had a turn.

Special support
Accompany any child who is severely visually impaired but encourage them to listen for the sound and tell you when you are getting near. Give verbal and visual clues to any child whose hearing is severely impaired, for example, 'It's behind the red curtain', 'It's under the blue cushion' and so on. You might find the signs for basic colours depicted on page 48 helpful here.

Extension
Encourage older children to make maps and treasure trails to help others to find the hidden box.

LEARNING OBJECTIVE FOR ALL THE CHILDREN
● to use everyday words to describe position.

INDIVIDUAL LEARNING TARGETS
● to locate objects using sound 👁
● to locate objects using colour. 👂

LINKS WITH HOME
Ask parents and carers to lend any musical boxes that they have. Encourage the children to handle them gently and to enjoy listening to and talking about the tunes that they play.

LEARNING OBJECTIVE FOR ALL THE CHILDREN
● to begin to relate subtraction to 'taking away'.

INDIVIDUAL LEARNING TARGET
● to join in a simple number rhyme.

👁 👂

Five little aliens

Group size
Ten to 30 children.

What you need
Five number cards, approximately A4 size, numbered 1 to 5.

What to do
Carry out this activity with the children during your regular circle time, music time or number time. Sit together in a circle and introduce this action song. Sing it to the tune of 'Twinkle, Twinkle, Little Star' (Traditional), or chant it as a rhyme.

> Five little aliens travelled this way,
> Looking for adventure on a rainy day.
> They flew round and round and one lost its way
> Landed at *(name of town or village)* and decided to stay.
>
> *Hannah Mortimer*

Hold up five fingers for the first line. Move your flat hands round and round in the air for the next two lines (to represent flying saucers). Then bring one of your hands down to 'earth' on the final line. Add the name of your town, village or locality in the final line. In the next verse, start with 'four little aliens' and so on, and finish when all the aliens have landed.

Invite five children to hold up the number cards in order with the numbers facing the other children. Invite 'Number 5' to sit down during the first verse, 'Number 4' during the second and so on. As you sing each verse, challenge the children to read the next number, staying in order, to decide how many are left.

Special support
Sit close to the child that you are targeting so that you can prompt and help when they find the correct number of fingers or read the number cards. Children with sensory impairment are often more willing to give an answer in a one-to-one situation than in a group. Once you have an individual answer, support them and help them to feel confident as they tell everyone in the group.

Extension
Let older children sing the song starting with 'Ten little aliens'. Design alien hats for the children holding the number cards to wear.

LINKS WITH HOME
Ask the children to teach this rhyme to their parents and carers so that they can sing it and practise counting on their fingers at home.

LEARNING OBJECTIVES FOR ALL THE CHILDREN
● to count reliably to ten
● to respond to everyday words which describe position.

INDIVIDUAL LEARNING TARGETS
● to become aware of where their body is in space 👁
● to respond to abstract vocabulary. 👂

LINKS WITH HOME
Ask parents and carers to help their children to learn the simple positional words such as 'in', 'on', 'under', 'in front' and 'behind' by setting their children challenges with a teddy and a box, for example, 'Can you put Teddy behind the box?'.

Sally Pally says...

Group size
Six to ten children.

What you need
A silly clown hat or wig; adult helper.

What to do
Move into an open space and tell the children that you are going to play a game. Tell them that you are going to dress up as a silly clown called Sally Pally who is going to ask them to do silly things. Explain to the children that they must not do as 'Sally Pally' says – only what you say! Have a go in order to show them what to do. Put on your hat and make a funny face. Say, 'Sally Pally says put your hands on your head'. Most of the children will do this, regardless of what you have said! Take a few turns until they have grasped the rules. Use your adult helper to signal to the children that they must not listen to 'Sally Pally'!

Now remove your hat and say 'I say put your fingers behind your ears!'. Praise all the children for listening and for doing this.

Alternate playing 'Sally Pally' and yourself as you give the children different instructions. Ask your helper to assist you as you support the children in listening to the key words and especially the position words such as 'under' or 'on'. Try to make Sally Pally's suggestions more and more unlikely, for example, 'Sally Pally says put your tummy on top of your head!'.

Special support
Be aware that this game does become rather noisy. It is therefore best carried out with smaller numbers of children. Some children with sensory impairment might find laughter and noise alarming, so stay close to them to keep the game fun.

Extension
Let older children take turns at being Sally Pally.

KNOWLEDGE AND UNDERSTANDING OF THE WORLD

This chapter focuses on exploring, predicting, looking, listening and finding out. Children with sensory impairments need extra support in order to compensate for loss of incidental learning.

LEARNING OBJECTIVE FOR ALL THE CHILDREN
● to identify some features of events they observe.

INDIVIDUAL LEARNING TARGET
● to play with imagination in a familiar context.

At home

Group size
Two children at a time.

What you need
A shoebox; cardboard; scissors; scraps of fabric; wallpaper offcuts; glue; assortment of craft materials and tools; small-world people.

What to do
This activity is ideal for a parent helper or personal support assistant to carry out with the child that you are targeting and their friend. Set up a craft table somewhere quiet and well lit. As always, make sure that the adult is sitting on the child's best side for hearing. Show the children the shoebox, opened and turned on to its side. Share the idea of making a tiny doll's house, 'astronaut's pod', 'fire station' or whatever catches the children's imagination.

Be led by the children's ideas, but help to organize them, for example, if they decide to paint the interior of the box. They might ask you to cut windows or doors, which you can hinge down one side by folding the card. They might like to paper the walls or stick up curtains and blinds. Talk about furniture and fittings. What would the dolls, astronauts or firefighters like in their home? Experiment together as you find ways of making tables, chairs, beds and so on from your craft materials or construction kits. Be prepared for this activity to carry on for some time, and give the children plenty of time to play together with their construction once it is completed.

Special support
Stay close to the children during the construction phase in order to help them to realize their ideas and select resources and methods. Use your commentary to make the communication flow easily between the two children, adding signing or rephrasing what has been said, if necessary, in order for the children to understand and respond to each other.

Extension
There is no limit to the things that you can design, plan and invent using a shoebox!

LINKS WITH HOME
Let each child make a shoebox 'house' to take home to play with. Suggest that parents and carers ask their children to show them in detail what they have made.

Our eyes

Group size
Four children at a time.

What you need
A picture book about eyes and vision such as *The Senses* by Paul Bennett (*Body Works* series, Belitha Press); long, soft scarves; dark blanket or cover.

What to do
Sit with the children and share the picture book together. Talk about how our eyes help us to see. Pair the children together and ask them to take it in turns to look at each other's eyes. What colour are they? Tell them that the coloured part of the eye is called the iris. Can the children see the dark part in the middle? Say that this is called the

pupil. Explain to the children that the eye is shaped like a ball but that they can only see the front part of it. The pupil lets in the light, and nerve cells at the back of the eye carry messages to the brain.

Ask the children if they can see in the dark. Put a dark blanket over all of you. Can you still see clearly? Explain that you cannot because there is no light going into your pupils.

Now let the children take turns with a partner to cover their eyes with their hands for a slow count of ten, then remove their hands. Invite the other child to look at their partner's pupils. What do they notice? Explain that the pupils get larger in the dark in order to let more light in.

Finally, tie a scarf over one of the partners' eyes in each pair while the other partner leads them around. Encourage the 'leaders' to tell the 'followers' what they are walking past and what obstacles are in the way.

Special support
Carry out this activity prior to welcoming a child with visual impairment into the group. This will help the children to understand and respect the child's needs. Talk about useful ways in which the children can help their new friend, by saying their names as they approach, picking up obstacles from the floor and putting toys away in their correct places.

Extension
Look at a model of an eye and talk about spectacles and lenses.

LEARNING OBJECTIVE FOR ALL THE CHILDREN
● to find out and investigate some features of living things.

INDIVIDUAL LEARNING TARGET
● to have their individual needs understood. 👁

LINKS WITH HOME
Emphasize in a newsletter to parents and carers how important regular eye checks are for their children as they begin to read and write.

56

KNOWLEDGE & UNDERSTANDING OF THE WORLD

LEARNING OBJECTIVE FOR ALL THE CHILDREN
● to find out and investigate some features of living things.

INDIVIDUAL LEARNING TARGET
● to have their individual needs understood. 👂

Our ears

Group size
Six or eight children.

What you need
A picture book about ears and hearing such as *The Senses* by Paul Bennett (*Body Works* series, Belitha Press); long, soft scarves; shaker; bells; recorder; drum.

What to do
Sit with the children and share the picture book together. Talk about how your ears help you to hear. Pair the children together and ask them to take turns to whisper very softly into each other's ears. How quietly can they whisper so that their friend can still hear them? If they turn away to whisper, can their friend hear them then? Explain that they can hear because their ear funnels the sound down a tiny tube called the ear canal, and inside their head there are nerve cells that send the messages to the brain so that they can hear.

Listen to high sounds such as those produced by a shaker, bells and high notes on a recorder. Then listen to low sounds such as those of a drum and low notes on a recorder. Make high and low sounds with your voices. Ask the children to close their eyes. Can they hear even if their eyes are closed? Tie scarves loosely over their ears, then whisper to them all, 'Hello'. Can they hear what you are saying? Can they see what you are saying with your mouth? Talk about how important it is to speak clearly and to face anybody who cannot hear very well.

Special support
Carry out this activity prior to welcoming a child with hearing impairment into the group. This will help the children to understand and respect the child's needs.

Extension
Encourage older children to play a game of 'Chinese whispers' around a circle with each child whispering a message to the next.

LINKS WITH HOME
Ask parents and carers to play whispering games with their children at home. Can they listen to and remember a simple challenge such as 'Look out of the kitchen window?'.

LEARNING OBJECTIVE FOR ALL THE CHILDREN
● to investigate objects and materials using touch.

INDIVIDUAL LEARNING TARGETS
● to identify an object by touch 👁
● to describe an object using touch. 👁 👂

What am I?

Group size
Four to six children.

What you need
A large drawstring bag; several objects of distinctive shape or feel such as a ball, teddy bear, shoe, hairbrush, handbag and so on; large cardboard box.

What to do
Sit down in a circle together. Show the sighted children your collection of objects and pass these around for themn to feel. Name the objects as you pass them around so that any child with visual impairment can link the name to the feel. Now place all the objects into the large cardboard box and remove it from the circle. Tell the children that you are going to put just one thing into the bag. Do this inside the box so that the children cannot see.

Now bring the drawstring bag back to the circle and sit down again. Reach inside and start describing what you can feel, for example, 'It's small, it feels very rough at one end, it has a handle…'. Encourage the children to guess what it is that you are describing, then draw out the hairbrush to show them that they were correct. Repeat for new objects, allowing each child to take a turn at describing. This may take a little practice so that the children do not 'give the game away' too quickly! If a child finds the description hard, use questions to prompt their words.

Special support
Repeat a child's descriptions clearly to any child with impaired hearing, using signing, radio aid or lip reading, if this is appropriate. If necessary, carry out this activity on a one-to-one basis with any child who is visually impaired so that they practise thinking of appropriate describing words.

Extension
Invite older children to select suitable objects.

LINKS WITH HOME
Send an 'ideas sheet' to parents and carers so that they can play the game with their children at home.

Twinkle, twinkle

Group size
Large group, then three or four children at a time.

What you need
Pictures of stars and the moon; reflective card; luminous star and moon stickers; scissors; pen; glue; dark covers, rug and chairs; black sugar paper; strong torch; nappy safety pins.

What to do
Sit down with all the children and talk about the stars and moon, showing them your pictures. Ask, 'What shines in the sky at night-time?' and 'What happens to them during the day?'.

Carry out a craft activity with three or four children. Outline moon and star shapes on the back of reflective card and invite the children to cut these out. Spread out a large sheet of black sugar paper on the table and invite the children to stick on their moons and stars to make a 'night sky'. Add luminous star and moon stickers.

During the next session, set up some chairs and a dark cloth in a darkened corner of the room to make a den. Leave the entrance open. Pin the sugar paper, star-side down, to make a ceiling, and place a comfortable rug for lying on. The den needs to be approximately two metres high. Invite the children to lie on their backs in the den (with their feet sticking out) and to take it in turns to use the torch to illuminate the 'stars' and 'moons' in the 'night sky'. Stay outside the den and ask them to describe to you what they can see.

Special support
Reflective paper and card can be useful craft materials for children who have limited vision. Sometimes, brightly reflective surfaces are much easier for them to see if these are well lit in a darkened space such as the den made above or their bedroom.

Extension
Talk with older children about different planets and add a few of these to the 'night sky'.

LEARNING OBJECTIVE FOR ALL THE CHILDREN
● to observe and find out about some features in the natural world.

INDIVIDUAL LEARNING TARGETS
● to turn towards light 👁
● to find simple words to describe what is seen. 👂

LINKS WITH HOME
Ask parents and carers to point out the moon and stars to their children on the next clear evening.

LEARNING OBJECTIVES FOR ALL THE CHILDREN
● to investigate objects using smell
● to observe and find out about plants.

INDIVIDUAL LEARNING TARGET
● to join in using their sense of smell.
◉

Herb garden

Group size
Four to six children.

What you need
The photocopiable sheet on page 91; window-box or large plant pot; potting compost; herbs as shown on the photocopiable sheet.

What to do
Decide whether you are going to make an indoor or an outdoor herb garden, and be guided by a garden centre or shop as to the best varieties of herbs to buy. Remember to check for any food allergies or dietary requirements.

Gather the children around to look at your collection of herbs and encourage the children to sniff them. If appropriate, wash a little parsley, mint and chives for them to taste. Explain that herbs are special leaves that you can eat and that they are used in cooking to make things tasty. They are also used in medicines because herbs can be good for you. Talk about the smells and the tastes.

Suggest to the children that you make a herb garden. Encourage them to help as you prepare the compost and plant the herbs. Mint needs to stay within its own pot under the earth or the roots will invade everything else. Invite the children to help with the watering over the next few weeks. If you are gardening outside, look for a place that is not too hot and not too cold, not too wet and not too dry. Talk with the children about the reasons for this.

Special support
Enjoy the fragrances and smells with the children and find words to describe them.

Extension
Prepare a herb salad together when your garden has grown.

LINKS WITH HOME
Give each child a copy of the photocopiable sheet to take home. Ask parents and carers to use the sheet to point out herbs in shops and gardens to their children and smell them together.

LEARNING OBJECTIVES FOR ALL THE CHILDREN
● to investigate objects using their sense of smell
● to talk about features they like and dislike.

INDIVIDUAL LEARNING TARGET
● to feel included and to develop a sense of smell. ◉

LINKS WITH HOME
Ask parents and carers to talk to their children about familiar smells in the kitchen at home. Can the children guess what is being prepared for tea?

Scent box

Group size
Three or four children at a time.

What you need
A set of opaque containers with screw-top lids such as used coffee jars, biscuit tins and tea canisters; different sources of smell such as coffee, tea, herbs, cocoa, cheese, spices and scents such as empty perfume or cologne bottles and bath oils; table; two coloured mats; two pieces of A4 card; pen.

What to do
Set up a range of similar-looking containers from which children can remove lids and smell the contents – for example, place some loose coffee, tea leaves, spice or cocoa in the bottom of each container. Leave the top off used perfume bottles and place one bottle in each container. Aim for approximately six different smells. You may wish to use food smells one day and perfume another. Make sure that you wash your containers well after using each content.

Take two pieces of A4 card and draw a smiley face with 'I like these smells' on one, and a sad face with 'I do not like these smells' on another. Place the containers on the table and one card on each coloured mat.

Invite the children to visit your smell table and sort the containers into smells that they like and smells that they do not like. Carry out this with one child at a time, talking about why they have chosen in that way. Invite the children to work in groups to sort the smells as this will encourage them to talk and discuss them between themselves.

Special support
Help a child with visual impairment by providing hand-over-hand support when opening the jars, if necessary. If a child is anxious about smelling the containers, do not insist that they do so.

Extension
Encourage older children to identify familiar smells and tell you what they are.

Clever concepts

Group size
Two children at a time.

What you need
An old suitcase; selection of items of different textures, colours, weights and sizes.

What to do
Choose the items for your suitcase carefully, for example, a man's shoe, a baby's shoe; a brush, a comb; a plastic pan scourer, a piece of sponge; a large red ball, a small yellow ball; two stacking rings of different size and colour; a length of ribbon, some Velcro; a wooden spoon, a metal spoon. Choose them as examples of the concepts that you wish to reinforce such as big/small, red/yellow, rough/smooth, wood/metal, long/short, heavy/light and so on.

Place the suitcase in front of the children and invite them to rummage through and explore its contents. Then set challenges in as natural a way as possible. As you play together, invite the children to give you a smooth object, or ask if there is a metal spoon or a small ball and so on. Encourage the children to use their own words to describe the contents.

Special support
This is a useful activity for reinforcing concept words for children who have sensory impairment. Carry it out for encouraging a child with visual impairment to name objects so that they have the opportunity to link words with touch. Leave the contents of the suitcase the same for a while so that the children can return to the case and explore it several times.

Extension
Find new and interesting objects together to add to your suitcase.

Ice cubes

Group size
Six to 12 children.

What you need
The photocopiable sheet on page 92; fridge with a freezer compartment; two ice-cube trays; jug of water; five cereal bowls.

What to do
Gather the children together and talk about hot things and cold things. What happens when water gets very, very cold? Talk about snow and ice and keeping warm outdoors. Does anyone know how to make ice? Show the children your ice-cube trays and let them watch as you fill them with water. Where will you put them now? Take the trays away to place one in the freezer compartment and one in the ordinary fridge. Ask the children to predict what will happen next. Check the trays

approximately every 15 minutes and talk about the changes that you can see. Take care to handle the ice-cube trays yourself with a cloth so that the children do not get ice burns.

When you have made the ice cubes in the freezer compartment, bring them out and remove them. Place one ice cube in each of the five bowls, then place the bowls in different areas of the room: put one near to a radiator, one on a window sill, one in a dark corner, one on a table and one in the fridge. Invite the children to make predictions about which one will melt first. Encourage the children to check the ice cubes every five minutes and to tell you what is happening. Watch the clock so that you can measure the time that it takes for the cubes to melt.

Give each child a copy of the photocopiable sheet and ask them to record the results by colouring in the appropriate ice cube as it melts. Were their predictions correct? Why?

Special support
Encourage the children to use the words 'freeze' and 'melt'. Let any child with visual impairment handle the melting ice cubes once they have been out of the freezer for a little while, warning them that they are very cold. Can they feel what is happening?

Extension
Invite the children to make fruity ice cubes with fruit juices and pieces of real fruit.

LEARNING OBJECTIVES FOR ALL THE CHILDREN
● to find out about freezing
● to look closely at change.

INDIVIDUAL LEARNING TARGETS
● to join in using the sense of touch 👁
● to use the words 'melt' and 'freeze'. 👂

LINKS WITH HOME
During wintertime, ask parents and carers to show their children what happens when puddles freeze and to point out the frost on trees and plants.

LEARNING OBJECTIVE FOR ALL THE CHILDREN
● to investigate flour and bread-making using all their senses.

INDIVIDUAL LEARNING TARGET
● to join in an activity fully, using every sense available to them. 👁 👂

LINKS WITH HOME
Give parents and carers a copy of the photocopiable sheet so that they can try the recipe at home. Buy the fresh yeast from bakers or traditional grocers in quantity so that you can send small amounts home.

Fresh bread

Group size
Four to six children at a time.

What you need
The photocopiable sheet on page 93; 300g strong white flour (plus extra for dusting); 5g sugar; 10g fresh yeast; 170ml lukewarm water; 10g salt; 10g lard; butter; jam; radiator; large bowl; greased breadloaf tin; oven; cooling rack; bowls of soapy water; towels; aprons; adult helper.

Preparation
Check for any food allergies or dietary requirements.

What to do
Carry out this activity at the beginning of your session. Help the children to put on aprons and follow the recipe on the photocopiable sheet as you read it, which involves plenty of handling, rubbing, squishing and kneading.

Ask each child to wash and dry their hands carefully, then let them feel the ingredients. Talk about how they feel and the textures. Follow the recipe and encourage the children to mix the ingredients together. Ask questions such as, 'Is it still sticky?', 'Are your hands floury enough?', 'What does it smell like now?' and so on. Help the children to wash their hands again carefully after handling the dough. Encourage them to go and play while you carry on kneading the dough, but ask them to return from time to time to see how you are getting on. Talk about the dough rising and how the air makes the holes inside the bread. When the dough is ready, take it away to bake it safely.

When the bread has cooked, tap the base to see if it sounds hollow and cooked. Place it on a wire cooling rack when it comes out of the oven and wait for it to cool a little before taking it back to the children. Cut it open and eat it with butter and jam while it is still warm, and enjoy the smell and taste!

Special support
Children with visual impairment will enjoy handling the ingredients. Provide a running commentary as you make the bread and as they help to mix the dough.

Extension
Let older children make buns and plaits.

PHYSICAL DEVELOPMENT

This chapter focuses on confidence, control, imagination, tracking and co-ordination. Children with visual difficulties will need your support to develop confidence when moving, as they may find it hard to know where their bodies are in space.

Keeping track

Group size
Two children at a time.

What you need
A plain wall or a screen made out of white paper; overhead projector; acetate sheets; washable projector pens; cushions.

What to do
Set up the overhead projector in a darkened area of the room. Place it so that it projects down to a low level with the plain wall or screen at floor height. Put some cushions on the floor in front of the screen and invite the children to kneel on them. Switch on the projector bulb and have fun making shadows with your fingers and hands. Ask the children to sit back as you move a point across the screen by using the tip of

your finger on the projector plate. Can they follow it with their eyes all the time? Make your point move smoothly from left to right and back again, then round in complete circles, first one way, then the other. Praise the children for looking very carefully.

Now invite the children to kneel down low while you move a point across the screen. Challenge the children to point with their own fingers and try to keep them on top of your shadow.

Finish by tracing some shapes with a pen on the projector, inviting one child at a time to trace it with their finger on the screen. Practise the movements involved in simple letter formation in this way.

Special support
Stay close to any child that has visual difficulties, encouraging them to track the shadow carefully. You may have to adjust light sources and background lighting to make this possible, depending on the child's difficulties. Assess visual tracking skills during the activity.

Extension
Using a paper screen, give each child a pen and invite them to form the letters as you do so on the projector, following your movements.

LEARNING OBJECTIVE FOR ALL THE CHILDREN
● to move eyes and fingers with confidence and control.

INDIVIDUAL LEARNING TARGET
● to practise visual tracking. 👁

LINKS WITH HOME
Encourage parents and carers to practise visual tracking at home. Ask them to shine a torch on a bedroom wall and to invite their children to keep it in focus by following it with their eyes all the time.

LEARNING OBJECTIVE FOR ALL THE CHILDREN
● to move with control and imagination.

INDIVIDUAL LEARNING TARGET
● to develop body awareness. 👁 👂

This way, that way

Group size
Six to 20 children.

What you need
A floor cushion for each child.

What to do
Arrange the cushions in a circle on the floor and invite the children to come and sit down. Teach them this action song based on the traditional rhyme and tune of 'Good Night Ladies' (Traditional).

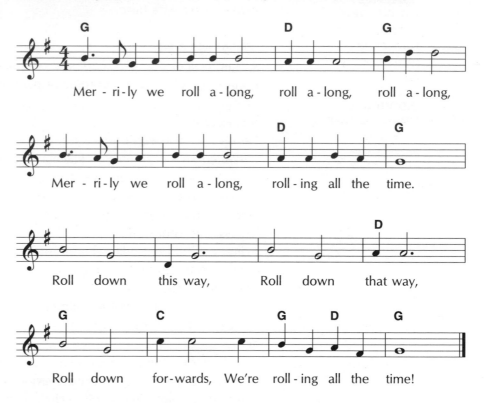

Sing the first two lines quickly, rolling your hands around each other. Sing the third line, rolling your hands down slowly and steadily to the left. Put your hands out to keep your balance. Then roll them down slowly to the right, again keeping the movement controlled and balanced. Sing the words slowly as you roll right down forwards towards the floor and back again. Repeat several times, taking it gradually faster.

Special support
Sometimes children with visual impairment have difficulties in knowing where their bodies are in space. This activity will encourage balance and control. The cushion will help them to know which position to return to after each roll. Stay close to support and encourage them.

Extension
Invite older children to sing pirate songs with rocking and rolling movements as you 'toss about on the sea'.

LINKS WITH HOME
Encourage parents and carers to practise balancing skills at home. Ask them to challenge their children to walk on their toes, on their heels, on the insides of their feet and on the outsides of their feet. Can they still keep a straight line?

LEARNING OBJECTIVE FOR ALL THE CHILDREN
● to move with confidence and in safety.

INDIVIDUAL LEARNING TARGET
● to move confidently despite limited vision.

Centipede march

Group size
Eight to 20 children.

What you need
An open floor space, indoors or outdoors; large drum.

What to do
Invite the children to form a long line. Ask each child to face forwards and to put their hands on the shoulders of the child in front, then to walk slowly forwards. Tell the children that they look like a long centipede and explain what it is. Ask them to stop so that you can count out loud together all their legs.

Now take the lead, asking the child behind you to put their arms around your waist. Encourage all the children to copy what you do. Jump forwards slowly with both feet together. Then stop and waggle one leg out to the side, then the other. Now bend down and stoop as you hobble forwards. Hop twice, then march with big strides. Praise the centipede for moving its legs so well!

Finally, beat the drum as you march around the room chanting:

> We're doing the centipede march!
> We're doing the centipede march!
> One, two, one, two,
> We're doing the centipede march!
>
> *Hannah Mortimer*

Slow the rhythm right down, then build it up steadily. Challenge the centipede legs to keep in time with you!

Special support
Make sure that a child with limited vision follows close behind you so that you can provide a firm lead and help to steady them, if necessary.

Extension
Invite older children to take a turn as the head of the centipede and let them choose the actions for everyone else to copy.

LINKS WITH HOME
Ask parents and carers to point out a centipede to their children when they see one in their garden or yard.

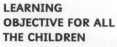

LEARNING OBJECTIVE FOR ALL THE CHILDREN
● to show awareness of space, themselves and others.

INDIVIDUAL LEARNING TARGET
● to move in response to a key word. 👁 👂

Fish, chips, bangers and mash

Group size
Six to 20 children.

What you need
A large open space; tape recorder or CD player; music tape or CD.

What to do
Take the children to the open space and introduce the game. Tell the children that every time they hear you say 'Fish!', they should crouch down. If they hear 'Chips!', they should run around. If you say 'Bangers!', they should jump in the air. If they hear you say 'Mash!', they should stand absolutely still. Practise with you doing the movements as well so that the children can copy you. When they begin to know what to do, see if they can do it without your help.

When you feel that the children are ready, put on a musical tape for everyone to dance to. Stop the music from time to time and call out one of the four words. Praise the children for remembering the actions and also for moving safely without bumping into each other.

Special support
Start with two words and build up to four. Stay close to a child with severe visual difficulties to avoid rough and tumble. Give a clear visual signal for a child who has hearing difficulties when you stop and start the music.

Extension
Invent new words and new actions for everyone, for example, think of a different word for the four walls of a sports hall, encouraging the children to run to that wall when they hear the word.

LINKS WITH HOME
Explain to parents and carers that you have been encouraging the children to listen carefully to words. Suggest that they say their child's name and make eye contact before they give important instructions to their child.

SPECIAL NEEDS **in the early years:** Sensory difficulties

LEARNING OBJECTIVE FOR ALL THE CHILDREN
● to move and balance with control.

INDIVIDUAL LEARNING TARGET
● to develop body awareness. 👁

On the way to market

Group size
Six to ten children.

What you need
A PE bench or similar; large straw hat; carrot.

What to do
Place the straw hat at one end of the PE bench and a carrot just in front of it. Explain to the children that this is Dobbin the carthorse and that he is big and strong enough to take you all to market to buy your shopping. Show the children how to sit astride the bench, all facing the same way.

Say that you are all riding Dobbin and that you are on the way to market! Teach this chant to the children.

> Plod, plod, plod, plod, we're on the way to market!
> Dobbin the horse is plodding along
> We're on the way to market!
>
> Trot, trot, trot, trot, we're on the way to market!
> Dobbin the horse is trotting along
> We're on the way to market!
>
> *Hannah Mortimer*

Ask each child to place their hands on the waist of the child in front as you sway slowly from side to side to the rhythm of the 'plods'. Move slowly and carefully so that you stay balanced and do not fall to one side. Praise the children for riding Dobbin so carefully. In the second verse, jog gently up and down from a sitting position. Praise the children, then return to a steady 'plod' as you sway and balance again.

Special support
Placing hands on waists will give a child with visual impairment a sense of where they are in space and will help them to stay steady. Let the child sit behind an adult helper.

Extension
Invite older children to take shopping baskets to 'the market', stop to find something to bring home, then ride back home. Can they still balance with something in their hands?

LINKS WITH HOME
Give each child a copy of the photocopiable sheet on page 94 so that they can share the rhyme with their parents or carers and enjoy colouring the illustration.

LEARNING OBJECTIVE FOR ALL THE CHILDREN
● to move with confidence and imagination.

INDIVIDUAL LEARNING TARGETS
● to move their bodies in different ways 👁
● to know what position their body is in at any one time. 👁

LINKS WITH HOME
Ask parents and carers to play with their children games that encourage them to develop body awareness, such as *Twister* (Tri-ang).

Monster shapes

Group size
Ten to 20 children.

What you need
An open space; tape player or CD player; tape or CD of fantasy music such as the *Harry Potter* film soundtrack by John Williams (Golden Stars).

What to do
Move into the open space and explain to the children that you are going to dance like monsters.

Play the music and enjoy a minute of moving in imaginative and monstrous ways. Then stop the music and ask the children to sit down. Take the first turn yourself. Announce loudly, 'I met a monster and it looked JUST LIKE THIS'. Then put your body into a spiky or scary shape and provide a commentary about what you are doing, for example, 'It had big arms and long claws that circled around like this, and huge shoulders, and its legs were crouched like this, and it had a ferocious expression on its face like this'.

Replay the music as the children take up new ideas in their monster dance. Stop the music and invite a child to play the body-sculpting game, starting with the same words. Use your own descriptions to describe the monster's shape to the others. Continue until all the children who want to have had a turn, then encourage all the children to take up a monster shape whenever the music stops.

Special support
Give a clear visual signal when the music starts and stops for a child who has severe hearing impairment. Encourage a child who has severe visual impairment to feel the body sculpture gently and use your own words to describe the shapes that the child has made. Invite that child to make their own monster shape and again use your words to describe what they are doing for them.

Extension
Ask older children to talk about the shape that they are making.

LEARNING OBJECTIVES FOR ALL THE CHILDREN
● to recognize the changes which happen to their bodies when they are active
● to show awareness of space.

INDIVIDUAL LEARNING TARGET
● to practise guided running. 👁

LINKS WITH HOME
Emphasize in your newsletter to parents and carers the importance of regular exercise for everyone. Have a sponsored 'Walk to the group' day when everyone walks to, or parks a little way away from, the setting.

Run around

Group size
Even number of children up to 30.

What you need
An open space; elastic-waisted clothes such as tracksuit bottoms or woollen scarves (one for each pair of children); tape recorder or CD player; music tape or CD; coloured hoops (four less than you have children).

What to do
Take the children into the large space. Help each child to find a partner without anyone feeling left out. Lay the hoops down on the floor and tell the children to dance around them without touching them while the music plays.

When the music stops, ask the children to stand still inside a hoop so that there is just one or two children in each hoop. Play the music for approximately 30 seconds. Ask the pairs of children that are sharing a hoop to sit down together when the music stops. Continue removing hoops until each child has paired up with another.

Now invite the children to play a running game with their partners. Encourage one child to take the lead while the other puts a hand gently into their waistband. Alternatively, tie a scarf around their waist to make a belt to hold on to if there is no waistband. When the child in front runs, the child behind should also run. When the leader stops, the follower should try to stop, too. Look out for pairs who do this well and let them show off to the others. Let the children take it in turns to be the leader and the follower, running and stopping all around the space.

Special support
'Guided running' is a helpful means of taking exercise for people with severe visual difficulties. Invite the child that you are targeting to be the follower.

Extension
Encourage older children to play a shadowing game in which the follower must shadow all the movements of the leader.

LEARNING OBJECTIVES FOR ALL THE CHILDREN
● to use a range of equipment
● to move with confidence, control and in safety.

INDIVIDUAL LEARNING TARGET
● to move with confidence and enjoyment in a defined space. 👁

LINKS WITH HOME
Suggest to parents and carers that they fill a large tub of water outside on a hot day. Encourage them to provide a selection of small objects and to talk with their children about those that sink and those that float.

Jellyfish fun

Group size
Four children at a time.

What you need
A warm day; paddling pool; lukewarm water; plastic balls; coloured latex gloves; elastic bands; indelible felt-tipped pen (adult use); soft towels; chairs; plastic bucket.

What to do
On a warm day, set up your paddling pool and fill it with lukewarm water. Let the children enjoy playing in the pool for a little while and have fun being together. Then suggest that they play some water games. Give the children the latex gloves to play with and share the fun as they try filling them with water or air. Prepare some 'jellyfish' together by filling the gloves with water. Bind the ends firmly for the children with elastic bands and use the indelible pen to mark eyes on the bodies. Remember to check for latex allergies. If there are any, use lightweight plastic balls instead of latex gloves.

Make your jellyfish swim and dive. Hold the plastic bucket and encourage the children to throw the jellyfish or plastic balls out of the pool into the bucket. Then hide them in the pool and challenge the children to find the red one, the blue one and so on. Invite the children to try to locate them with their toes, or sit on them! Make some jellyfish with air in – do they still sink? Which ones float? Use the time when the children are getting dried as an opportunity to talk together and socialize.

Special support
A paddling pool is a good way of providing a confined area in which a child with severe visual impairment can feel confident and move freely. Stay close to the children to inspire confidence, sharing and pleasure.

Extension
Add a selection of objects that sink or float into the paddling pool with the children.

PHYSICAL DEVELOPMENT • PHYSICAL DEVELOPMENT • PHYSICAL DEVELOPMENT

LEARNING OBJECTIVE FOR ALL THE CHILDREN
● to travel around, under, over and through equipment.

INDIVIDUAL LEARNING TARGET
● to develop confidence in moving in different ways.
👁 👂

LINKS WITH HOME
Encourage parents and carers to help their children to practise climbing and balancing skills safely at the local playground.

Getting there

Group size
20 children.

What you need
Large floor space; selection of large apparatus such as a plastic tunnel, mats, benches, hoops, large cardboard boxes, covers and rugs; two large teddy bears, one wearing a large 'a' and one a large 'b', made from a piece of card and string to hang around their neck.

What to do
Place 'a' bear and 'b' bear at opposite corners of the room. Scatter your apparatus on the floor in between. Gather the children together, sitting around 'a' bear and introduce this chant.

> There are twenty ways of getting there,
> to move from a to b.
> There are twenty ways of getting there,
> Just watch us and you'll see.
> We can tunnel, climb or run,
> And we're different, every one.
> There are twenty ways of getting there,
> to move from a to b!
>
> *Hannah Mortimer*

Let the children take turns to find a new way of moving from teddy to teddy, using the apparatus in different ways. Use your own running commentary to describe the movements in the style of a sports commentator, for example, 'She's crawling underneath the rug, now she's climbing over the bench, now she's hopping towards the tunnel' and so on. Emphasize the action words. Repeat the chant approximately every five children. Cheer when all the children have reached 'b' bear and have fun playing with the equipment for a while.

Special support
Move alongside a child with severe visual impairment, or encourage a child with mild difficulties from the side.

Extension
Ask older children to help you to select and set up the obstacle course.

LEARNING OBJECTIVE FOR ALL THE CHILDREN
● to show awareness of space, of themselves and others.

INDIVIDUAL LEARNING TARGET
● to locate a space using sound. 👁

Sounds like 'mice'!

Group size
Up to eight children.

What you need
Your usual play spaces, indoors or outdoors; adult helper.

What to do
This is a simple variation of the traditional party game 'Sardines', in which one person hides and the others join them as they find the hiding place. The play area needs to be quiet for this game. You could play it indoors when the rest of the group are outside or busy elsewhere.

Tell the children that you and the child that you are targeting are going to pretend to be little mice hiding in a hole and they will hear little squeaks to help them to find where you are. Ask the adult helper to wait with the children while you go and hide with the child that you are targeting. Choose somewhere to hide, out of immediate sight, that all the children can eventually fit into! The helper and the children should count very slowly to 20 and cover their eyes while you hide.

Then the helper should send two children at a time to search, leaving an interval between each pair. Make little squeaks from your hiding place. When the first two children have found you, encourage them to join you and help with the squeaks. Continue until all the mice have arrived at the 'hole'. Have several turns so that different children can be hiders or seekers.

Special support
If a child has a hearing loss involving certain frequencies, select the best sound for the hiders to make, for example, a low growl, a low note on a recorder, or a drum beat.

Extension
Hide two 'mice', one with some jingle bells and one with a shaker. Challenge older children to find the mouse hole with the sound of the shaker, or find the mouse hole with the sound of the bells.

LINKS WITH HOME
Suggest to parents and carers that they play this as a party game at home, explaining that it will provide excellent practice for listening skills!

CREATIVE DEVELOPMENT

This chapter provides ideas for developing children's creativity and imagination using art and craft, music, sounds and colours. Children with hearing and visual difficulties will be limited in the senses that they can use in these activities and will need you support.

LEARNING OBJECTIVE FOR ALL THE CHILDREN
● to explore colour, texture and space in three dimensions.

INDIVIDUAL LEARNING TARGET
● to explore the water tray. 👁 👂

LINKS WITH HOME
Suggest to parents and carers that they add bath foam, some plastic containers and bottles to the bath water at home, so that their children can enjoy pouring and emptying. This is creative and fun, and will also help the children's understanding of quantity.

Water music

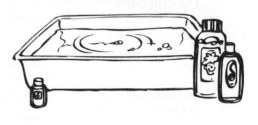

Group size
Three or four children at a time.

What you need
A water tray with a transparent base; selection of water-tray toys, containers, pourers and funnels; rubber-covered 'heavy-duty' outdoor torch that is safe if splashed (adult use); spotlights (optional); tape recorder or CD player; tape or CD of calm music such as Handel's *Water Music*; small plastic bottles with selection of fragrant moisturizing bath foams; food colourings; dark covers.

Preparation
Set up the water tray with lukewarm water and arrange any spotlights to provide low-level light at a safe distance from the tray. This can be very effective if you darken the corner around the tray with dark covers. Arrange the bath-foam bottles where they are easily accessible on a nearby table. Be aware of any children who have eczema and check that the solutions that you are using will not affect the children adversely.

What to do
Play the music and invite the children to join you in your water grotto. Splash gently as you add a few drops of different food colouring and let the children enjoy the colour changes. Show them the bath-foam bottles and let them add foams and perfumes to the water and enjoy the fragrance. Use the torch to make the water shine from underneath the tray, but do not let the children play with this.

Continue to support the children's play as they introduce the selection of toys and pourers into the water tray. Talk about the effects, textures and smells that you are enjoying together.

Special support
Use light and contrast to encourage best use of any limited vision. Encourage a child with hearing impairment to enjoy and talk about the sights and textures, and make sure that they can still see your face when you are talking together.

Extension
Talk about why it is dangerous to use electricity near to water and explain to the children why you used a special torch.

LEARNING OBJECTIVE FOR ALL THE CHILDREN
● to respond in a variety of ways to what they see and feel.

INDIVIDUAL LEARNING TARGETS
● to move and regard their fingers 👁
● to enjoy exploring touch and colour. 👁 👂

LINKS WITH HOME
Suggest to parents and carers some musical keyboard and early computer games such as those in the RNIB toy catalogue (see page 95) for their children to play at home, to encourage isolated finger movements and hand control.

Finger fun

Group size
Two or three children at a time.

What you need
Fluorescent or iridescent finger-paints and finger-paint paper (available from NES Arnold, see page 96); paint palettes; large window at child height or dark paper; aprons; washing-up bowls; towels.

What to do
Select approximately five different-coloured finger-paints and put them into paint palettes. Arrange the paints and paper on a table near to a child-height window if you are going to try glass-painting. Help the children to put on aprons. Show them the finger-paints and enjoy isolating one single finger or thumb carefully and dabbing each into a different colour. Encourage the children to look at their fingers. Are they all different colours?

Now make finger-tip dabs on to the dark paper or a large window. Continue to explore and experiment with the paint, making colourful creations but also enjoying and talking about the process – for example, the children may decide to make a garden full of blooms, a jazzy pattern or a firework display on the window. Show the children how to wash their hands between using different colours if they want to keep the colours separate. Bear in mind that they can wipe and reuse the finger-paint paper if they wish to.

Special support
Children with visual impairment may need bright colour contrasts to appreciate colour. Admire their pictures under a fluorescent light.

Extension
Try finger-painting a repetitive pattern, for example, 'dab, dab, stroke', 'cross, dab, dab' and so on, and encourage the children to do the same. Can they make a colourful pattern to go around the window or a mirror?

LEARNING OBJECTIVE FOR ALL THE CHILDREN
● to explore colour, form and space in three dimensions.

INDIVIDUAL LEARNING TARGETS
● to play alongside other children
● to talk about what they see and feel.
👁 👂

Junk tray

Group size
Up to four children at a time.

What you need
Dry water tray; selection of objects such as an egg-box, rustly greaseproof paper, foil, chocolate-box tray, new washing-up brush, zip, pheasant-tail feather, fir and pine-cones, conkers, cotton reels, ping-pong balls, cardboard tubes, bicycle bell, purse with a stud popper, wind-up alarm clock, pastry shape cutters, sponge, plastic monsters and animals, large coat buttons, wooden spoons and meat tenderizer (wooden mallet with rough ends available from kitchenware shops).

What to do
Encourage the children to visit the tray and simply enjoy exploring, feeling and talking about everything that they find there.

If you are going to leave your junk tray up for a few days, keep some new items aside so that you can change them slightly each day.

Special support
This activity is ideal for a younger child with sensory impairment. The space is clearly defined for a child with visual impairment so that nothing gets lost, and there are plenty of opportunities for linking concepts and words for a child with hearing difficulties.

Extension
Invite older children to go on a 'junk-tray hunt' around the room and suggest to you objects that would be useful.

LINKS WITH HOME
Invite parents and carers to help their children to look out for interesting natural objects to go in the tray.

LEARNING OBJECTIVE FOR ALL THE CHILDREN
● to respond in a variety of ways to what they see, smell, touch and taste.

INDIVIDUAL LEARNING TARGET
● to taste and talk about. 👁 👂

Jelly on a plate

Group size
Four to six children.

What you need
Packets of different-flavoured sugar-free jellies; transparent jelly moulds; saucepans; cooking hob (away from the children); wooden spoons; plates; bowls; spoons.

Preparation
Check for any allergies or dietary requirements.

What to do
Start the activity by chanting the action rhyme 'Jelly on the Plate' (Traditional) with the children.

> Jelly on the plate, jelly on the plate,
> Wibble-wobble, wibble-wobble,
> Jelly on the plate!

Wobble all over as you chant it. Mime placing the jelly carefully on the floor and reaching for your spoon to take a big spoonful. Repeat the rhyme with the words 'Jelly on my spoon'. Finish by miming a big mouthful, then say, 'Jelly in my tum!'.

Suggest to the children that you make some jelly together. Encourage them to wash and dry their hands carefully. Let them work in pairs to break up the jelly cubes and place these in a saucepan. Talk about what you will do next, introducing the words 'heat' and 'melt'. Ask the children to wash their hands again as you take the pans away to melt the jelly, following the directions on the packets.

Next, show the children the melted jelly and let them watch as you pour it into the moulds. Place the moulds somewhere cool, then when they have set, gather the children together again as you turn them out on to the plates. Enjoy a tasting session together and invite the children to talk about which one they enjoyed the most.

Special support
There are plenty of opportunities for touching, smelling and tasting during this activity. Introduce simple describing words for each sensation such as 'sticky', 'flavour', 'strawberry taste' and so on.

Extension
Encourage older children to work out how they might create a stripy jelly. Add fruit and other garnishes.

LINKS WITH HOME
Explain to parents and carers that you have been thinking about tastes. Encourage them to talk to their children about tastes at home and to try to find simple words to describe them.

LEARNING OBJECTIVES FOR ALL THE CHILDREN
● to recognize and explore how sounds can be changed
● to recognize repeated sounds.

INDIVIDUAL LEARNING TARGETS
● to copy a simple sound with instruments 👁
● to copy a simple vibration with a drum. 👂

LINKS WITH HOME
Ask the parents or carers of a blind child to encourage road-safety awareness by helping their child to listen to road sounds – for example, a car stopping might indicate a crossroads ahead, or a car slowing down might mean that there is a side road. Invite the parents or carers to encourage them to listen for buses slowing down at bus stops, 'green men' beeping at crossings and so on.

Echo, echo

Group size
Ten to 20 children.

What you need
A selection of percussion instruments including bongo drums.

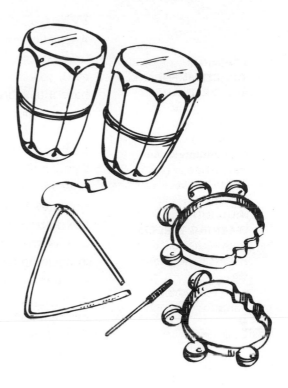

What to do
Carry out this activity with the children during your regular music time or circle time. Use an earlier session to teach the children that when you play your instrument, they can play, too, but when you stop playing yours, the children should stop as well.

Sit down all together in a circle on the floor. Place a selection of percussion instruments in the centre of the circle and invite pairs of children, by name, to come and choose an instrument. Save a large drum for yourself. Play your drum loudly for a few seconds, then stop. Praise the children for playing and stopping, too.

Explain that you are going to play a copying game. The children should listen to what you do and then do the same. Say, 'My turn!' loudly and make one beat. Now say, 'Your turn' (following a continuous rhythm with your beat), and repeat the sound with them as they copy. After a few turns, stop playing the echo with the children as they should now understand what to do. Keep it simple, for example, two slow beats, three quicker ones; a rapid flurry of beats; a long beat and a quick beat, and so on. Then move around the circle, giving each child a simple sound to echo on their instrument.

Special support
If a child's hearing is severely affected, let the child place a hand on the surface of the drum as you beat so that they can feel the vibration. Now encourage them to copy that vibration, using a gentle hand-over-hand prompt if necessary.

Extension
Invite older children to provide sounds for others to copy. Carry out the activity echoing back nonsense words!

CREATIVE DEVELOPMENT • CREATIVE DEVELOPMENT • CREATIVE DEVELOPMENT

LEARNING OBJECTIVES FOR ALL THE CHILDREN
● to use their imagination in art and design
● to explore colour and texture in two and three dimensions.

INDIVIDUAL LEARNING TARGETS
● to select collage materials using touch 👁
● to use describing words for materials. 👂

LINKS WITH HOME
Suggest that parents and carers carry out this activity at home. Encourage the children by saying that you would be interested to see the finished products!

Touch collage

Group size
Four to six children.

What you need
A selection of collage materials that are interesting to touch and handle, for example, fur, sandpaper, corrugated card, feather, Velcro, shiny card, sequins and so on; selection of backing papers and materials that have interesting and contrasting textures, for example, corrugated card; scissors; glue; trays.

What to do
Plan carefully how you are going to arrange the materials. Involve the children in deciding how you are going to sort and arrange them, for example, by sorting some by texture and some by appearance. Suggest to the children that they make a picture that is really interesting to feel. Show them an example as you select and snip pieces of material and glue them on to corrugated backing paper. Invite the children to close their eyes and touch your picture. Ask, 'What does it feel like?'.

Now invite the children to handle and feel the collage materials and to plan what backing paper and collage pieces they would like to use. Let each child place their choices in a separate tray so that everything can be easily located. Support them as they make their creations.

Special support
Children with visual impairment need working materials that are well contrasted, for example, dark on light or vice versa. Both collage materials and backing paper should have interesting and contrasting textures. Provide a commentary in the child's usual method of communication so that a child with hearing impairment links words with textures, colours and shapes.

Extension
Plan and create an attractive and tactile wall frieze for an entrance lobby or quiet area.

Glamorous spectacles

Group size
Three or four children at a time.

What you need
Sheets of white A4 paper; sheets of A1 coloured card; washable felt-tipped pens; glitter; glue; scissors; elastic bands; sticky tape; different-coloured Cellophane.

What to do
Start by giving each child a sheet of white paper on which you have drawn the outline of their face. Encourage them to add hair, eyes, a nose, a mouth and so on, then invite them to design and draw a fabulous pair of spectacles to go on to their face. Help each child to make their design by drawing on to the card the approximate shape of the spectacles that the child would like, and add two side arms that will eventually hold the spectacles on with elastic bands (see illustration).

Help each child to cut out the spectacles, then invite them to decorate them with the pens, spread some glue and add glitter. Let the children choose the colour of Cellophane that they would like in the lenses. Place the spectacles on one side to dry.

When the spectacles are dry, cut out the centre of the lenses and stick a piece of Cellophane behind the frames in place for each eye. Invite the children to have a parade wearing their glamorous spectacles!

Special support
Have a selection of story-books and picture books in your setting that reflect a range of abilities in their pictures, for example, children who wear spectacles.

Extension
Talk with older children about why people need to wear spectacles and how they help them to see.

LEARNING OBJECTIVES FOR ALL THE CHILDREN
● to respond in a variety of ways to what they hear
● to match movements and sounds to music.

INDIVIDUAL LEARNING TARGET
● to understand where their body is in space. ◉

LINKS WITH HOME
Bubble wrap is an ideal material to use for dancing and stamping on with bare feet. Suggest to parents and carers that they play some music at home and let their children perform a bubble-popping dance.

One-child band!

Group size
Six to 12 children.

What you need
Single jingle bells; ribbon; strips of Velcro; sewing kit (adult use); selection of percussion instruments.

Preparation
This activity is based on a 'one-man band' – a busking musician who has several instruments attached to his body and who can sing and play his own band all at the same time. Sew single bells on to loops of ribbon (for looping around fingers) or lengths of Velcro (for attaching to arms or legs). You may be able to adapt some of your other instruments so that they can be looped or attached by belts to a moving child. The idea is for a child to become a musical instrument or 'one-child band'.

What to do
Share your idea with the children and enjoy dressing one of them up with attached musical instruments or bells. Tuck a shaker into a pocket or two. Encourage the child to move and enjoy making a jangling and swishing sound.

   Now sit in a circle and invite the 'one-child band' to move slowly around the outside while the other children shut their eyes and point to the sound. Ask them to open their eyes from time to time and invite them to say whether they were correct or not.

Special support
When two or three children have had a turn, let the child that you are targeting have a turn. Hold their hand as they move around the circle. Play a version with big boots and a stamping march on a wooden floor for a child who has hearing difficulties. Can the children hear and feel the direction of the boot stamps?

Extension
Buy toe socks (available from high-street shops) and sew bells on to the toes for a musical pair of socks.

CREATIVE DEVELOPMENT · CREATIVE DEVELOPMENT

LEARNING OBJECTIVE FOR ALL THE CHILDREN
● to explore light, form and change.

INDIVIDUAL LEARNING TARGET
● to use limited vision to identify similarities and differences. 👁

Rainbow pairs

Group size
Six children, then two at a time.

What you need
The photocopiable sheet on page 89; six sheets of A4 reflective card of different textures and colour sheens (available from craft shops); scissors; pens; table; black table-cloth; angle-poise lamp or spotlight.

What to do
Sit down with the children and explain that you would like their help to prepare a game. Let them admire the shiny card and talk about the colours and effects. Use the photocopiable sheet as a template to draw six basic shapes on to the back of each reflective card. Cut the card into six so that there is one shape on each piece of card. Invite the children to cut out the shapes, helping them if necessary. Give each child the shape that is just within and just beyond their present capability, with squares being the easiest and crosses the most difficult. Cut out the rest of the shapes, naming them as you do so. Thank the children for their help and invite just two to stay and play the game.

Spread a dark cloth on the table. Shine a bright light on it, and deal out the shapes to the three of you. Help each child to arrange a pile of shapes in front of them. Then play a game of 'Snap!', taking it in turns to place one card at a time, shiny side up, on to the cloth. Place them beside each other rather than on top. As soon as there is a pair, encourage the children to shout, 'Snap!', and place that pair to one side. In this version of the game, work as a team and everyone is a winner!

Special support
Make a point of showing the matching shapes to a child with limited vision and ask whether they are the same or not. You may need to use the cards first to teach what 'same' and 'different' mean.

Extension
Help older children to use the shapes to make reflective shape mobiles that turn and shimmer in the light.

LINKS WITH HOME
Encourage parents and carers to ask their children to point out three things that are shaped like a circle and three things that are shaped like a square on their way home from the setting.

LEARNING OBJECTIVE FOR ALL THE CHILDREN
● to express and communicate their ideas using a widening range of materials.

INDIVIDUAL LEARNING TARGET
● to add a sound or visual effect to a story. 👁 👂

LINKS WITH HOME
Rehearse the whole story together, then perform it to parents and carers at home time.

Sound tale

Group size
Six to 20 children.

What you need
A selection of percussion instruments; sound-making materials such as crinkly paper, washboard and wooden spoon, thunder sheet, coconut shells, blowing tubes, steam-train whistle and so on; picture book of a familiar story; adult helper.

What to do
Choose a short story that the children are very familiar with, such as 'The Three Billy Goats Gruff' or 'The Three Little Pigs' (Traditional). Remind the children of the main story line, using your picture book. Now invite them to choose some sounds to go with the story.

Place a selection of instruments in the centre of the circle, together with the other sources of sound effects.

Talk about the story and encourage a discussion and experimentation so that the children can select the best sounds to go with the story. This may include inviting the children to select instruments that make 'happy' music, 'cross' music, 'scary' music, 'sleepy' music and so on. If you cannot find the best sound in the circle, look around the room for ideas or try experimenting with your voices. Look for opportunities for the children to use the musical instruments creatively and combine them in new and interesting ways.

Special support
Always make sure that each child has a role to play, even if they find it hard to think creatively themselves. Use an adult helper to prompt the children and encourage them to come in at the correct time.

Extension
Record your story, complete with sound effects, on to tape and use it in the listening corner to accompany the picture book.

Individual education plan

Name:	Early Years Action/Action Plus

Nature of sensory difficulty:

Action	Who will do what?
1 Seeking further information	
2 Seeking training or support	
3 Observations and assessments	

4 Encouraging learning and sensory development
What exactly are the new skills that we wish to teach?

How will we teach them?

What opportunities will we make for helping the child to generalize and practise these skills throughout the session?

How will we make sure that the child is fully included in the early years curriculum?

Help from parents or carers:

Targets for this term:

How will we measure whether we have achieved these?

Review meeting with parents or carers:

Who else to invite:

Jack and the Beanstalk

Who's my friend?

Ropes and trees

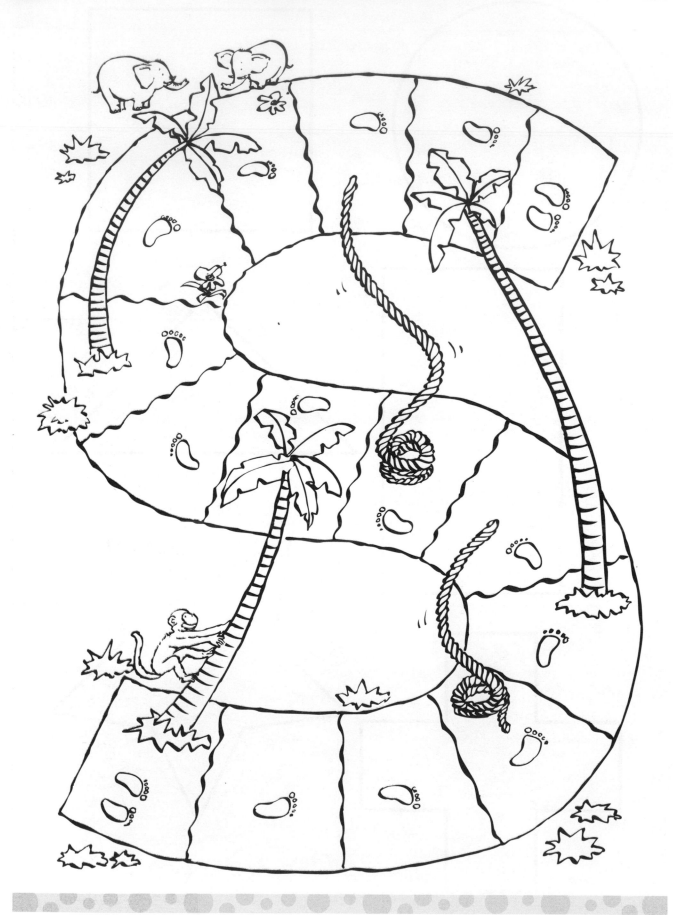

 SPECIAL NEEDS **in the early years:** Sensory difficulties

Herb garden

mint

chives

parsley

basil

thyme

sage

Ice cubes

We placed our ice cubes in five different places:

Near the radiator

On the window sill

In a dark corner

On a table

In the fridge

SPECIAL NEEDS **in the early years:** Sensory difficulties

Fresh bread

What you need
300g strong white flour
10g fresh yeast
10g salt
5g sugar
170ml lukewarm water
10g lard
radiator
mixing bowl
cling film
greased breadloaf tin
oven

What to do

● Warm a large bowl on a radiator, then tip in the flour, yeast, salt and sugar.

● Measure the water and pour it into the bowl.

● Mix the ingredients together with your hands.

● Add the lard and rub into the mixture.

● Sprinkle flour on to your hands and knead the dough, lifting and stretching it.

● An adult should knead the dough for ten minutes until it is smooth and no longer sticky! Roll it in a ball, cover with cling film and leave near to a radiator.

● When the dough has expanded, knead again for three minutes then leave to stand again for half an hour.

● Knead the dough again and fold it over several times.

● Leave the dough to settle for ten minutes, then place in a greased breadloaf tin for an hour, then bake 35 minutes at 220°C/425°F/Gas Mark 7.

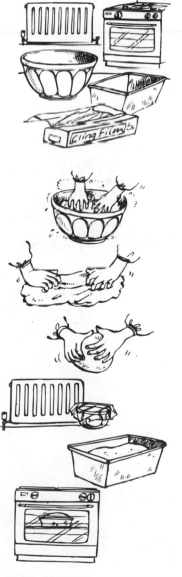

On the way to market

Enjoy this rhyme with your child and colour the picture together.

Plod, plod, plod, plod, we're on the way to market!
Dobbin the horse is plodding along
We're on the way to market!

Trot, trot, trot, trot, we're on the way to market!
Dobbin the horse is trotting along
We're on the way to market!

Hannah Mortimer

RECOMMENDED RESOURCES

ORGANIZATIONS AND SUPPORT GROUPS

● The *CaF Directory* of specific conditions and rare syndromes in children with their family support networks can be obtained on subscription from Contact a Family, 209–211 City Road, London EC1V 1JN. Tel: 020-76088700.

● National Association of Toy and Leisure Libraries, 68 Churchway, London NW1 1LT.

● National Blind Children's Society, NBCS House, Market Street, Highbridge, Somerset TA9 3BW. Tel: 01278-764764.

● National Library for the Blind, Far Cromwell Road, Bredbury, Stockport SK6 2SG. Tel: 0161-3552000.

● Royal National Institute for the Blind (RNIB), 105 Judd Street, London W1H 9NE. Tel: 020-73881266. Send sae for resource list and toy catalogue.

● Royal National Institute for Deaf People (RNID), 19–23 Featherstone Street, London EC1Y 8SL. Tel: 0808-8080123.

● Sense (for people with deaf-blindness and associated disabilities), 11–13 Clifton Terrace, Finsbury Park, London N4 3SR.

BOOKS FOR ADULTS

● *All Together: How to Create Inclusive Services for Disabled Children and their Families* by Dickens and Denziloe (National Early Years Network)

● *Focus on Foundation Including Children with Impaired Vision in Early Years Settings.* Available from RNIB, address above.

● *Get Up and Go: Fun ideas to Help Visually-impaired Children to Move Confidently* available from RNIB, address above.

● *Index for Inclusion: Developing Learning and Participation in Schools* by Booth, Ainscow, Black-Hawkins, Vaughan and Shaw (CSIE). Available from Centre for Studies on Inclusive Education, Room 2S 203, S Block, Frenchay Campus, Coldharbour Lane, Bristol BS16 1QU. Tel: 0117-3444007.

● *Look and Touch: Play Activities and Toys for Children with Visual Impairments* (RNIB and the National Association of Toy and Leisure Libraries). Available from RNIB, address above.

● *More Quality Circle Time* by Jenny Mosley (LDA). Ideas on using circle time in nursery and Reception classes, including the use of puppets, drama and guided imagery.

● *The Music Makers Approach: Inclusive Activities for Young Children with Special Educational Needs* by Hannah Mortimer (NASEN). Available from The National Association for Special Educational Needs, 4–5 Amber Business Village, Amber Close, Amington, Tamworth, Staffordshire B77 4RP. Tel: 01827-311500.

● *Special Needs and the Early Years Provision* by Hannah Mortimer (Continuum)

BOOKS FOR CHILDREN

● *Friends Going Swimming* by Diane Church (Franklin Watts). Rowan is deaf and likes to go swimming.

● The Magination Press specializes in books that help young children to deal with personal or psychological concerns. Send for a catalogue from The Eurospan Group, 3 Henrietta Street, Covent Garden, London WC2E 8LU. Tel: 020-72400856.

● *Making it! Zoo Keeper* by Eleanor Archer (Franklin Watts). Katy the zoo keeper is deaf and this story-book tells how she communicates with her friends and colleagues.

WEBSITES

● The Department for Education and Skills (DfES) (for parent information, Government circulars and advice including the SEN *Code of Practice*): www.dfes.gov.uk

● Formative Fun sell a range of early learning toys including the tactile 'smart frame' bead-threading maze: www.formative-fun.com

● RNIB: www.rnib.org.uk

● RNID: www.rnid.org.uk

● The Writers' Press, USA, publish a number of books for young children about a range of SEN: www.writerspress.com

EQUIPMENT AND RESOURCES SUPPLIERS

● Acorn Educational, 32 Queen Eleanor Road, Geddington, Kettering, Northants NN14 1AY. Tel: 01536-400212. Supply equipment and resources for early years and special needs.

● KCS, PO Box 700, Southampton SO17 1LQ. Tel: 01703-5843134. Specialist tools for making computer equipment accessible to all children.

● LDA Primary and Special Needs, Duke Street, Wisbech, Cambridgeshire PE13 2AE. Tel: 01945-463441. Supply a range of transparent pattern blocks, shapes and counters for use with an overhead projector.

● RNIB toy catalogue. Features the LEGO 'Musical Apple'.

● NES Arnold, Excelsior Road, Ashby Park, Ashby-de-la-Zouch, Leicestershire LE65 1NG. Tel: 0845-1204525. Supply fluorescent and iridescent finger-paints and finger-paint paper.

● Step by Step, Lee Fold, Hyde, Cheshire SK14 4LL. Customer careline: 08451-252550. Supply toys for all special educational needs.

ORGANIZATIONS THAT PROVIDE TRAINING COURSES

● Children in Scotland, Princes House, 5 Shandwick Place, Edinburgh EH2 4RG. Tel: 0131-2288484. Courses in early years including SEN.

● The Council for Awards in Children's Care and Education (CACHE), 8 Chequer Street, St Albans, Hertfordshire AL1 3XZ. Tel: 01727-847636.

● The High/Scope Institute UK, 192 Maple Road, Penge, London SE20 8HT. Tel: 020-86760220.

● Makaton Vocabulary Development Project, 31 Firwood Drive, Camberley, Surrey GU15 3QD. Tel: 01276-61390. For information about Makaton sign vocabulary and training.

● National Children's Bureau, 8 Wakley Street, London EC1V 7QE. Tel: 020-78436000. Many seminars and workshops on children and SEN.

● National Early Years Network, 77 Holloway Road, London N7 8JZ. Tel: 020-76079573. For customized in-house training.

● National Portage Association, PO Box 3075, Yeovil, Somerset BA21 3JE. Tel: 01935-471641. For Portage parents and workers, training in Portage and information on the 'Quality Play' training.

● Pre-school Learning Alliance, Pre-school Learning Alliance National Centre, 69 Kings Cross Road, London WC1X 9LL. Tel: 020-78330991. For information on DPP courses and their special needs certificate. Free catalogue, order form and price list of publications also available.